LADY JANE GREY

NINE DAY QUEEN OF ENGLAND

Lady Jane Grey
From an original portrait by Hans Holbein

From an Original Picture by Hans Holbein.

LADY JANE GREY

NINE DAY QUEEN
OF
ENGLAND

by

Faith Cook

EVANGELICAL PRESS

EVANGELICAL PRESS
Faverdale North, Darlington, DL3 0PH, England

e-mail: sales@evangelicalpress.org

Evangelical Press USA
P. O. Box 825, Webster, New York 14580, USA

e-mail: usa.sales@evangelicalpress.org

web: http://www.evangelicalpress.org

First published 2004
This edition 2005

British Library Cataloguing in Publication Data available

ISBN-13 978-0-85234-613-6   ISBN 0-85234-613-1

Scripture quotations in this publication are from the Holy Bible, Authorized/King James Version.

Printed and bound in Great Britain by:
Creative Print and Design, Ebbw Vale, Wales.

DEDICATION

To
Kim Fisher
my American friend, whose enthusiasm for
Lady Jane's story has been
a great encouragement

To visit Bradgate Park leave the M1 at Junction 22 and take the A50 in the Leicester direction. Turn left at the 1st roundabout for Newton Linford.

Glasgow

Edinburgh

Newcastle
Upon Tyne

Manchester

Bradgate Park

Leicester

Birmingham

Cardiff

London

CONTENTS

Preface and Acknowledgements

Bradgate Park – Leicestershire's premier country park! For almost twenty years this spacious country park with its riverside walk, its rocky outcrops, its undulating bracken-covered hills, and its mildly inquisitive deer, formed a significant part of our family life. From the mid-1960s until we left the Midlands it was to Bradgate that we returned again and again for family outings. And always the sight of the crumbling old ruins – all that remains of the palatial manor where Lady Jane Grey was born and brought up – lent a strange sobering ethos to the scene. Her pitiful and heroic story has long fascinated me and yet despite several requests I have hitherto felt unable to write about it.

Part of my reluctance to tackle such a record has lain in the complicated political intrigue that surrounded Lady Jane's life. For one who has often been called the 'Tudor Pawn', no simplistic story of the life and death of a sixteen-year-old would be adequate. To understand the tragedy and triumph of Jane's life it would be vital therefore to grasp the far-reaching political and religious changes that were shaking England at the time, as the effects of the Reformation touched a whole population, from the palaces strewn along the River Thames, to the Universities, the emerging towns and even the peasant cottages. I must therefore apologize in advance if some of my chapters appear at first to have little to do with Lady Jane. But, like a complicated jigsaw, with a degree of patience the pieces will all be found to fit together, giving a picture of a girl with outstanding natural abilities whose strength of character and remarkable faith shine out despite the darkness that often surrounded her.

Many accounts have appeared over the years; some present her in terms of stirring heroism, others as a sweet and innocent victim and more recently as an unfortunate but misguided religious prig. A number of novels have also been written, and also a film made, embroidering her story both with credible and often less than credible detail. In this account I have attempted to sift fact from fiction and present a sympathetic though realistic assessment of Lady Jane's personality and the events of her life.

I have been grateful for the help of my local library in obtaining books long out of print and to the Records Office for Leicestershire, Leicester and Rutland which houses much material difficult to obtain elsewhere. I am grateful also to Ralph Ireland for his careful checking of my work; to David Davies for his enthusiasm for this attempt and encouragement to persevere; and my particular thanks to Jack Milner for his visits to Bradgate Park on my behalf to take some of these evocative photographs. I would also wish to acknowledge the assistance given by Michael Harrison, Land Agent & Surveyor for the Park, whose detailed knowledge of the history of Bradgate has been most helpful. My grateful thanks also to the Evangelical Library for the historical portraits, to the British Library for the picture of Lady Jane Grey's prayer book, to Lara Eakins for the photograph of the engraving in the Tower, and to my daughter Esther Bennett for the photographs of the Tower sites. As always I would wish to acknowledge the invaluable help of my husband Paul.

Because the year 2004 marks the 450th anniversary of the death of Lady Jane, a new record of her life has also seemed appropriate. In days when absolute truth has become a casualty of our post-modern society, with its tolerance of everything except strong Christian convictions, the faith of Lady Jane Grey remains a challenge to us all. Her unswerving courage, even when the alternatives of life or death were set before her and depended upon the answers she gave, should not be forgotten.

Faith Cook
September 2004

CHAPTER ONE

BORN A TUDOR

On a mild Saturday afternoon in late spring the car park at Bradgate Park in the Charnwood Forest is crowded with vehicles: few spaces remain. Families with young children, the elderly in wheelchairs, energetic youths with footballs at their feet: it seems that the whole population of Leicester has converged on this one spot in the village of Newtown Linford. Here we may wander beside the slow-flowing River Lin, which winds its way through the park. We may stop to gaze at the red deer, with their deep brown coats and sharp antlers; or the smaller fallow deer with their dappled brown and fawn coats that roam fearlessly on the banks of the stream, or hide among the bracken that clothes the farther bank.

The gentle greens of spring add hopefulness and vitality to the scene. Even the gnarled old oaks appear to have a new lease of life. Amid the boundless acres of woodland and undulating hills there is room for everyone to relax and delight in the fresh springtime air. Only the strange old ruins of Bradgate Manor set apart on rising ground and the odd shape of some of the oldest of the oaks appear to tell another story.

How surprised would young Lady Jane Grey have been at such a scene. For Bradgate Manor, with its wide sweep of surrounding parkland, was once the home of a girl whose short life would leave her name stamped on the history books for many generations to come. More than four hundred and fifty years have elapsed since Jane studied, wrote letters and prayed in a small room in one of the ruined turrets – still to be seen today and known as 'Lady Jane's Tower' – or rode on horseback along these same paths and among these same woods. Called by some the 'Tudor pawn', maligned by others, or else depicted in terms of unrealistic eulogy, Jane remains one of the least understood figures of Tudor history. The scenes of her life were

Ruin of Lady Jane's Tower

played out in the arena of a frightening array of self-seeking, power-hungry noblemen, many involved in political intrigue with plot and counterplot merging to confuse and obscure the truth.

On the other hand, Jane was privileged to live in days when new light was dawning on Britain as the Reformation truths increasingly gained sway in the hearts of the people. Although the Reformation of the English Church was inextricably interwoven with events taking place in the royal courts and noble houses of the day, there was at the same time a secret and yet more significant work of God moving the minds and consciences of men and women which had its spring some twenty years before Jane was born in 1537.

In March 1516 Desiderius Erasmus,[1] a Rotterdam scholar, had published the New Testament for the first time in its original Greek language. Hitherto Latin translations of the Scriptures, derived from Jerome's[2] Latin Vulgate rendering, had been, in the main, the only versions available, and these were jealously guarded by the priests. Now hot off the Basel press, the Greek New Testament had been brought across the English Channel and had found its way into the English seats of learning – to the universities of Oxford and Cambridge. Side by side with an updated Latin version of the text, plus explanatory notes, Erasmus had placed the Greek original. By this single publication Erasmus, called the 'literary king' of the new learning that was sweeping Europe, had done more than he could ever have imagined. He had unleashed a power both divine and awesome – the power of the Scriptures – a dynamism that would liberate Europe from the spiritual chains that had shackled the nations for many centuries.

As copies of the Greek New Testament were passed from hand to hand in the universities, a number of scholars were profoundly affected by the truths they discovered within its pages. In their private rooms, in the corridors, lecture rooms and refectories, groups of students and even university Fellows could be found discussing the Scriptures and pondering the implications of the principles of the Reformation both on the church and on their own lives. In this way the Scriptures alone, almost without any other agent, had led to the conversion of men of the calibre of Thomas Bilney, Fellow of Trinity Hall, Cambridge, in 1521 – and through him Hugh Latimer in 1524, a preacher whose thunderous messages powerfully influenced the royal courts of two Tudor kings.

Lady Jane Grey had Tudor blood in her veins – she was the great niece of that most controversial and shrewd of English kings, Henry VIII. Her grandfather, Charles Brandon, Duke of Suffolk, a contemporary and close friend of the young Henry, had married Mary Tudor, Henry's youngest and favourite sister. Mary was attractive and spirited and it was no surprise that Charles Brandon had fallen in love with her. But marriage in sixteenth-century royal circles was not a question of choice or preference. Above all, it was a way of establishing power and prestige amongst neighbouring dynasties, securing the right allies and uniting against common enemies. And, in Henry's view, what better alliance could England have at that present moment than with neighbouring France? Hostilities between the two countries had recently been resolved and the threat of trouble with Spain was now the greater danger. So it was decided that the petulant and lively Mary, only twenty years of age and the beauty of the English court, was to be married to the ageing king of France, Louis XII.

Far from happy with such an arrangement, Mary herself had been increasingly enamoured with Charles Brandon, despite the fact that he was already twice divorced. But as far as her marriage was concerned, she had little choice in the matter. However, she did manage to gain one concession from her royal brother: upon the death of her prospective husband, the sick old French king, which was regarded as imminent in any case, she should be allowed to marry a man of her own choosing. Finally, with a handsome dowry paid and costly ensemble purchased, Mary was shipped off to France and married to the ailing king in October 1514. A mere three months later Louis XII was dead.

Henry VIII's initial concern was to oversee his sister's welfare in these new circumstances; his secondary concern, at least so Mary feared, was to arrange a further advantageous marriage for her. Astonishingly, Henry commissioned his friend Charles Brandon to cross over to France to secure Mary's interests and to bring her back to England once all the necessary protocol had been completed. Knowing Brandon's affections for Mary, he insisted that on no account was his friend to make any amorous approaches to his sister – clearly she was too valuable a national asset to be married off to an English nobleman. Whether Henry had any intention of honouring his earlier commitment to allow Mary a choice in the question of any subsequent marriage is certainly doubtful.

Mary too had little confidence in her brother's word and dreaded being married off to yet another foreign monarch. As soon as she saw Charles she begged him to marry her. Out of reach of the King and already captivated with the princess, Charles could no longer withstand her pleas. He broke his word to Henry and he and Mary were secretly married in Paris. It was an act that nearly cost him his head, for Tudor kings, particularly one as fiery as Henry VIII, did not like to be crossed by their subjects. To add to his transgression, it appears that Brandon's last divorce had not been finalized. A special dispensation from the pope, not hard to obtain for the wealthy, would be needed to legitimize a marriage that otherwise would have been bigamous.

For some months the princess and Charles Brandon, who feared for his life, waited in France. A letter from Mary to her brother is extant; in it she took upon herself the blame for the circumstances, explaining to Henry that 'I put my lord of Suffolk [Charles Brandon] in choice whether he would accomplish the marriage within four days, or else he would never have enjoyed me; whereby I know well that I constrained him to break such promises as he made your grace.' She concluded with a plea to the King that he would 'write to me and my lord of Suffolk some comfortable words'. After Henry's initial anger had cooled and with Thomas Wolsey, presently Archbishop of York, also acting as an intermediary, Charles Brandon was eventually forgiven and returned to England with Mary Tudor. A second ceremony was conducted on English soil to put the marriage beyond question. The couple set up home in East Anglia, although much of their time would be spent either at court in London or at Charles Brandon's London home, Suffolk Place, situated on the south bank of the Thames at Southwark. Before long, Charles Brandon and Mary were expecting their first child. Meanwhile, Katherine of Aragon, first wife of Henry VIII, was also pregnant once more. In the light of Katherine's sad catalogue of miscarriages and infants that had only survived a few days, it could well be that the child due to Charles Brandon and Mary would succeed to the throne of England. They named their infant, born in March 1516, Henry after his uncle, Henry VIII, which might well suggest that this was a distinct possibility in the minds of his parents. The likelihood of this receded, however, when it appeared that Katherine of Aragon's newly-born daughter Mary was likely to survive. A second child born to the Brandons in July 1517, only sixteen months afterwards, was given the name of Frances – probably to bolster relationships with the French court. Another daughter, Eleanor, born several years later, would complete the family.

Despite the fact that Katherine of Aragon's daughter Mary appeared a healthy enough child, the Queen had failed to produce the male heir that the King so urgently looked for to consolidate the Tudor claim to the throne. Katherine had formerly been the wife of his brother Arthur, who had died in 1502. Henry conveniently interpreted the death of most of Katherine's babies as a sign of God's displeasure with his marriage. But when his eyes fell on the Queen's vivacious young maid-of-honour, Anne Boleyn, Henry was even more determined to divorce Katherine. He became increasingly embroiled in a long battle with the pope for his marriage to be declared null and void so that he might marry Anne and hopefully gain a son to inherit his throne.

Far distant from these scenes of royal unfaithfulness and intrigue, a lonely exile had been toiling incessantly to provide his countrymen with a treasure that would be of lasting significance – the Scriptures in their mother tongue. As we have seen, Erasmus' Greek New Testament had profoundly influenced scholars and academics, but William Tyndale, who had studied first at Oxford and then Cambridge, had a new ambition burning in his soul. While working as a tutor to the family of Sir John and Lady Walsh at Little Sodbury Manor in Gloucestershire, he had begun to translate the New Testament from the Greek into the common language of the people. 'If God spares my life', he declared to the local clergy who disparaged and opposed his work, 'ere many years I will take care that a ploughboy knows more of the Scriptures than you do' – and this he did. Unable to continue his work in England for fear of arrest and even death, he fled with his unfinished manuscripts in 1524, sailing along the River Elbe to Hamburg in Germany.

Despite many setbacks to his endeavours, the fugitive translator toiled on and by 1526 the first copies of the New Testament in English were being smuggled back into England on merchant ships, hidden among bags of flour and other commodities. Copies were circulated surreptitiously and as the people read the word of God for themselves, the new spiritual light that had first begun to shine in the universities radiated ever more brightly in the land – but at a cost. Thomas Bilney, the Cambridge Fellow, who was among the first to embrace Reformation truths, refused to compromise his faith. He was burnt in 1531 at *Lollards' Pit* outside Norwich, crying out, '*Credo*'[3] as the flames licked around him. Two years later John Fryth, one who had acted as Tyndale's assistant in 'the work of translation, was chained up by the neck, hands and feet in Newgate prison and then taken out and burnt at Smithfield, tied back to back to the same stake with a tailor's apprentice boy.

Such persecution often ignites interest, and perhaps it was at this time that Charles Brandon himself was first influenced by the Reformation truths. He may well have purchased and read a copy of Tyndale's New Testament, although we do not know to what extent his commitment was yet anything other than nominal. Meanwhile his children, Henry, Frances and Eleanor, were growing up at the family home of Westhorpe Hall, not far from Bury-St-Edmunds. By 1533, the year of John Fryth's martyrdom, Frances (Charles and Mary's elder daughter) had reached the age of sixteen and her parents considered that it was time for her to be married. In fact her father already had a prospective husband in view. This was Henry Grey, Marquess of Dorset, nineteen-year-old son of a former friend. More importantly from Charles Brandon's point of view, such a marriage would link any children that his daughter and Henry Grey might have even closer to the throne of England, for this young man could trace his ancestry directly back to Elizabeth Woodville,[4] wife of Edward IV.

Described as 'a great dicer and swearer', Henry was a weak and unstable character with little to recommend him apart from his wealth and noble birth. Pleasure-loving and easily influenced, he also had one further problem to overcome before he could marry Frances – he was already engaged to be married to the Earl of Arundel's daughter. Reneging on his commitment, as happened all too often among these unprincipled status-seekers, he grasped at this new opportunity opening up before him – a marriage which would make him one of the foremost noblemen of the time.

Mary Brandon attended her daughter's wedding at Suffolk Place in London, but it would be her last visit to the capital. A sick woman, she died at Westhorpe shortly afterwards at the age of thirty-eight. A regal funeral followed but Charles, who had spent little time at home in those last years of her life, did not attend. Only months after his wife's death he remarried, but his choice was not some high-born lady of his own age – instead it was a fourteen-year-old girl, Catherine Willoughby, who had been living with his own family for the last five years. Catherine, a young person of fine character, had in fact been promised as bride to Henry Brandon, Charles and Mary's seventeen-year-old son. To discover that his father, at almost fifty years of age, had decided to take the girl himself and make her his fourth wife, must have been a severe shock to the young man. Charles Brandon's motive is thought to have been mainly financial; the royal funeral arrangements for his wife, following shortly after his elder daughter's dowry payments, had left him with money problems. However, his son only lived another year, dying shortly before the birth of his father's first child by Catherine – another son, ironically also named Henry Brandon.

Henry Grey, who had become the third Marquess of Dorset after his father died in 1530, owned numerous estates, but Bradgate, in the Charnwood Forest, only five miles from the City of Leicester, was the most important. Bradgate Manor, a rambling and attractive mansion, was begun initially by Henry's grandfather, Thomas Grey, first Marquess of Dorset who had forcibly re-housed the Bradgate villagers to improve the appearance of the approaches to his new home.

Charnwood Forest still remains an area of outstanding natural beauty, and has been incorporated within the newly designated *National Forest.* Once, however, its scattered woodlands joined to form dense luxuriant forest, covering a wide area from Loughborough in the north to Leicester in the south. The River Soar, a tributary of the Trent, formed an eastern boundary, subdividing into streams with an abundant supply of trout. Located in a spacious clearing within a natural valley stood the Manor House, built of reddish-orange brick, a feature of many later Tudor buildings but at that time a material rarely used since the Roman occupation. The multi-turreted mansion was surrounded by gardens thought to be among the finest in England. Formal terraces with herb, fruit and flower gardens, a fish pond and even a tiltyard built by Charles Brandon, all added to the impressive scene.

Here it was that Henry Grey brought Frances, his sixteen-year-old bride, in 1533. And in these splendid surroundings the young couple now began their married life, supporting their grandiose lifestyle with a staff of three hundred servants living on the premises. Possibly such a retinue of servants was needed, for Henry Grey, Marquess of Dorset, kept daily table for two hundred or more guests, regularly entertaining politicians, gentry, and even royalty. A man's status was judged by the provisions offered to his guests, and of this the Marquess was well aware. The long tables at which his company sat groaned under the weight of food piled upon them – venison from the park, peacock, pheasant and other delicacies – a meal could often last for three hours.

Frances was a stronger character than her husband. Coarse and domineering, she displayed much of her uncle Henry VIII's determined opportunism. Coupled with this, she soon exhibited a ruthless streak that would allow nothing to stand in the way of political ambition. Bradgate provided abundant opportunities for indulging Henry and Frances Grey's predominant interests: hunting deer, hawking, fishing and chasing game in the woods and valleys of the surrounding forest.

When a young son was born to the couple in 1535 their joy as well as ambition swelled to new heights. With Henry VIII's daughter Mary, by Katherine of Aragon, now declared illegitimate and excluded from inheriting the throne, there only remained Elizabeth, infant daughter of Anne Boleyn, between their newborn son and the throne of England. With a monarch as capricious as Henry VIII, who could tell whether Anne Boleyn might also fall from favour? But such aspirations soon came to nothing for Frances and Henry Grey's first child lived only a few months. A second child was born in 1536 and its life too, like that of so many infants of the time, was only brief.

At this very time a tragedy of immense proportions was unfolding far off at Vilvorde, near Antwerp. The noble translator of the New Testament, William Tyndale, was being tied to a stake to be first strangled and then burnt. Cruelly betrayed by one whom he had trusted as a friend and assistant in his endeavour to complete his translation of the Old Testament, Tyndale had been imprisoned in Vilvorde Castle for many months. His New Testament was now circulating freely, though still clandestinely, throughout England and had even found an entry into the King's own palace as Queen Anne Boleyn read its pages and believed its truths. 'Lord, open the King of England's eyes!' was Tyndale's dying prayer as the executioner tightened the rope that would rob that earnest Christian man of breath and England of one of its greatest citizens. It was to be a prayer God answered to an extent that Tyndale could never have guessed.

During that same year of 1536 the political stage was changing yet again. The lustful King had turned his gaze away from the sprightly Anne and was looking instead at twenty-seven-year-old Jane Seymour, one of Anne's maids-of-honour. Like Katherine, Anne had also failed to produce the male heir that Henry so desperately wanted: more than this she was proving to be a friend of the 'New Religion', as the Reformation with its evangelical doctrine was dubbed. Anne was using her influence to promote the circulation of Tyndale's New Testament, and in Henry's eyes, his wife was taking upon herself more authority in her position as Queen than he appreciated. Anne had many enemies among politicians and nobility alike, and once it was noted that the King was beginning to entertain the possibility of other liaisons, Anne's days were numbered. Her antagonists reasoned that it would not be hard to pin accusations of adultery on the Queen and this would give Henry the excuse he needed to indulge his new attachment. In her distress, as she realized the fateful future looming up before her, Anne suffered a miscarriage – the child was a boy.

Events followed on with a frightening degree of inevitability. Anne was duly framed and then accused of adultery on a number of counts. Soon she found herself arrested and imprisoned in the Tower. She protested her innocence to the last. In a final letter to the King, she wrote movingly, 'Let not your grace ever imagine that your poor wife will ever be brought to acknowledge a fault ... never a prince had wife more loyal in all duty and in all true affection.' She begged God to forgive her husband his sin against her and continued by urging clemency for those unfortunate men, co-accused with Anne, who would also die in order that the King might have his heart's desire. Confessing her sins, particularly the sin of ever marrying Henry in the first place when Katherine was his lawful wife, Anne cast herself on the mercy of God. On 19 May 1536 she was led out to her execution on Tower Green. She died bravely, as even her bitterest opponents admitted; and by her death she freed Henry to marry Jane Seymour. The day after Anne's execution the King announced his engagement to Jane and a mere two weeks later the two were married at Whitehall. Jane was then proclaimed Queen and plans set in motion for her coronation.

Such events sent shock waves throughout the land. Never before had a Queen of England been executed, and the speed of Henry VIII's remarriage left few in doubt of the underlying motive for Anne's condemnation. Anne Boleyn and Henry's young daughter Elizabeth, not yet three years old, was soon declared illegitimate and disinherited like her half-sister Mary. These events would have had profound repercussions in far-off Leicestershire. With no certainty that Jane Seymour would give Henry VIII an heir, any children that Frances and Henry Grey might have would now stand a high chance of inheriting the crown of England. Soon Frances realized that she was pregnant once more but at almost the same time she learnt from the court gossips that Henry's new Queen, Jane Seymour, was also pregnant.

At 8 o'clock in the morning of 12 October 1537 news broke in London that Jane Seymour had given Henry his long-wished-for heir. Two thousand salvoes boomed from the cannons at the Tower; bells rang madly and the streets were festooned with bunting in honour of the newborn prince. Bonfires were lit on the hilltops and ale or wine flowed freely from every tavern to celebrate his birth. The infant, named Edward, appeared healthy and prayers of thanksgiving were raised in churches throughout the land.

In the midst of all these celebrations another child was born, this time at Bradgate Manor in Leicestershire: a daughter to

Frances and Henry Grey whom they named Jane, probably in honour of the new Queen. Although they were doubtless disappointed at their child's sex the Greys yet focussed all their ambitions on this small baby girl with her auburn hair, so characteristic of the Tudors. Even if the birth of a prince might preclude their child from inheriting the throne, there was a high probability that their new daughter would be chosen as bride for Edward and therefore become Queen of England. There is every evidence that her parents were well aware of the potential for reflected glory vested in the future of this baby. But to be born a Tudor at this perilous juncture of English history was a poisoned chalice – as Jane would one day discover.

CHAPTER TWO

LADY JANE'S EARLY YEARS

L ondon's joy at the birth of its prince was suddenly muted. Although the baby's mother, Jane Seymour, had apparently been well enough to attend the christening of her son, alarming news soon spread around that the Queen had succumbed to an infection: clearly the dreaded puerperal sepsis – the scourge that took its deadly toll on so many young mothers at the time. Twelve days after the birth of the fair-haired prince his mother was dead. Henry could only comment sadly to the French King, Francis I, who had sent a message of congratulation, 'The divine providence hath mingled my joy with the bitterness of the death of her who brought me this happiness.'

Now all Henry's concern was poured into regulations for the welfare of the child, spoken of as 'His Majesty's most noble jewel'. Walls of the nursery at Hampton Court were to be scrubbed twice daily, all water must be boiled and any dish, spoon or article of clothing brought into the royal nursery had to be washed before it came near the infant prince. Henry had good reason to fear for he had created many enemies for himself, particularly among the Catholic party. Three years earlier he had dared to dispense with the papal authority over English church affairs thus making himself Supreme Head of the Church in England. Lest any should attempt to poison his son all food fed to the baby had to be sampled by others first.

More than a hundred miles north in the English Midlands, another baby was being carefully nurtured. Because Frances and Henry Grey spent more of their time at court in London cultivating the right connections than they did at their home in Bradgate they appointed Mistress Ellen, a kindly Scottish woman, to be Jane's nurse. Under her watchful eye Lady Jane, a title she carried as the granddaughter of the King's sister, gradually gained strength.

Two years later a second daughter Katherine was born, described as the beauty of the family with her auburn hair and strong appealing features; then in 1545 came Mary – a sadly deformed child whose humpback and unattractive appearance would have proved a bitter circumstance for parents as proud and ambitious as Frances and Henry Grey. Meanwhile young Prince Edward was making excellent physical progress. Henry delighted in his son, and made regular visits to the royal nursery at Hampton Court. A surviving picture of the child painted by the artist, Hans Holbein, shows Edward much like any healthy baby the world over, apart from his elaborate headgear and regal clothing. Careful records were kept of his development: 'My lord prince is in good health and is merry,' reported his nurse. 'His Grace hath four teeth, three full out, and the fourth appearing.' But despite all the attention, the child lacked a mother's love. 'I was brought up among the women,' Edward commented in later years.

In 1539, as his son approached his second birthday, Henry began to consider remarriage. In addition to any personal consideration there were political issues that made a further marriage desirable. The treatment meted out to Henry's first wife, Katherine of Aragon, had angered her nephew the Emperor Charles V who had vast dominions covering much of Europe. Added to this the 1534 Act of Supremacy that made the King Supreme Head of the English Church had further alienated Charles V who had now formed an alliance with his old enemy France. This placed England in a vulnerable position. Expediency therefore dictated that the King should marry a princess from one of the German Lutheran States. This would act as a counterbalance to the united powers of France and Spain and, in the event of any attack on England, would provide the country with necessary allies.

Yet despite the appeals of his right-hand man, Thomas Cromwell, Earl of Essex,[1] whose initiative lay behind the proposal, Henry VIII was less than happy about such a marriage alliance. He still espoused the Catholic faith and did not wish to subscribe to the Augsburg Confession, a condition for any political rapprochement with the Lutheran princes. But as Cromwell continued to press the advisability of such a marriage, Henry agreed that tentative enquiries should be made on his behalf.

Soon Cromwell heard that the Duke of Cleves' unmarried sister Anne appeared to be a suitable candidate for the position and he commissioned Hans Holbein to paint her portrait. When the King was shown the artist's miniature, representing Anne as an attractive young woman, he acquiesced to Cromwell's suggestion and even began to show a degree of enthusiasm for the scheme. But on meeting his bride-to-be when she arrived in Rochester on 1 January 1540, Henry took an instant dislike to what he saw. Although his outward behaviour was impeccable, he spent as little time in Anne of Cleves' company as he reasonably could and soon returned to Whitehall, complaining, 'I see nothing in this woman as men report of her.' Tall and thin, Anne appears to have possessed little beauty and even less compensating charm or accomplishments.

Despite this, and also the fact that the political map was changing yet again thus making an alliance with the Lutheran states now unnecessary, Henry felt obliged to go through with the wedding ceremony. But it was an unpromising situation and the marriage lasted little more than three months. By this time the King, encouraged by his Catholic nobles, had set his eyes on the lovely Catherine Howard, niece of the powerful third Duke of Norfolk, and soon became infatuated with her beauty. By means of his spokesman the King informed Anne of Cleves that her marriage with him was invalid. After providing several spurious reasons for the decision, Henry announced that he was suing for a divorce.

Anne had no wish to invite upon herself the same fate as Anne Boleyn had encountered and appears to have accepted the circumstances without demur. Settled with three palaces at her disposal and an annual income of £500, she slipped into semi-obscurity, probably grateful for an early release from a position both hazardous and unsuited to her background and temperament.

A far worse retribution awaited Thomas Cromwell. Catherine Howard's Catholic relatives had risen to power with her and many had old scores to settle with Cromwell and the evangelical or reforming party which he represented. A smear campaign began against the man whose popularity with Henry was already waning because of his ill-judged attempt to pressurize Henry into an alliance with the Lutheran princes, and his unfortunate choice of a bride for the King. Before long his enemies managed to persuade the King that this one in whom he had placed utmost confidence was in fact a heretic, and had supported heretics. Now Henry had an excuse for disposing of Cromwell. Conveniently forgetting all he had obtained from Cromwell's skilled negotiations, he soon signed the warrant for the arrest of the politician. His inevitable execution followed on 28 July 1540.

Apparently unaware of her previous flighty lifestyle Henry meanwhile hurried to claim his new bride, eighteen-year-old Catherine Howard. Doubtless he hoped that the honour he was bestowing on Catherine by making her his Queen would compensate for his large and less-than-attractive physique and for the disparity in their ages – he was already forty-nine. Henry's cup of happiness was now full. He doted on his young heir, Edward, and with a new and engaging wife anticipated further sons to consolidate the Tudor line.

With the Catholic party once more pre-eminent, Henry soon reverted to practices which he had abandoned while he had a Protestant Queen at his side. He attended Mass frequently and carefully celebrated all the Saints' Days in the church calendar. Religious ceremonies, which had been in abeyance while the influence of Cromwell and Archbishop Thomas Cranmer was uppermost, were reintroduced. Worse than this was the renewed persecution against quiet and honourable citizens for trivial 'offences' such as refusing to celebrate Mass when burying their dead. Edmund Bonner, Bishop of London, glad of fresh opportunities for crushing the progress of the Reformation, was responsible for the imprisonment and torture of many faithful Christians. One young man, John Porter, was caught reading the Scriptures aloud in a public place. Thrown into Newgate prison, he was cruelly tortured and finally murdered there eight days later.

Ever since Henry VIII's divorce settlement from Katherine of Aragon in 1533, his good will had see-sawed between the Catholics and the Evangelicals, now favouring the one persuasion and executing men and women of the other, and then reversing his policy as his circumstances changed. In reality Henry was a pragmatist and the party which promoted his own position best at any given point gained the greater influence. But despite the King's enthusiasm for his new Catholic bride, his happiness was short-lived. Catherine merely continued her capricious way of life, flouting her marriage vows with impunity. It was only a matter of time before the King discovered that his wife, whom he had called his 'jewel of womanhood and perfect love', was cheating on him, not just once but many times over. For Catherine the path from the Tower to the execution block on Tower Green was the sad but predictable end for such conduct. The terrified girl was executed on 13 February 1542. In his grief the King was now looking increasingly old and grey; one foreign ambassador described him as 'so sad, pensive and sighing'. He was over-eating as well, probably an attempt to alleviate his depression – and soon his bed needed to be enlarged to seven feet in width to accommodate his corpulent figure.

As we have seen, together with Catherine's exalted position had come the ascendancy of the Howard family, staunch supporters of the 'Old Religion'. So now with her fall came also the fall of the whole Howard family and the Catholic interest with it, as they were dismissed from positions of honour within his administration. Such events would have been closely watched by the Grey family in Leicestershire. Charles Brandon, Jane's grandfather who championed the Reformation truths, had entertained the King and his 'Rose without a Thorn' as he called

Catherine, shortly before the discovery of her infidelity was disclosed to him. Undoubtedly the swiftly changing scenario would have been noted carefully at Bradgate Manor.

By the time of Catherine's execution in 1542, Prince Edward had already been introduced to two stepmothers, neither of whom would have had the opportunity, time, nor possibly the inclination, to foster any relationship with the young prince. Both Edward and Lady Jane had now turned four years of age and their education had begun in earnest. If the Catholic party had retained power, it is highly probable that the men engaged to teach the prince and possibly also his Leicestershire cousin Jane would have been men of that persuasion. As it was, both Edward and Jane received their early education from tutors of evangelical principle. Dr Richard Cox, a well-reputed Cambridge scholar, headmaster of Eton College and more significantly friend of the Reformation truths, was Edward's first tutor.

For girls to receive an academic education was a novelty in the early sixteenth century – many considered that such learning was not suitable for them in view of the life most would lead. Others maintained that girls lacked the intellectual capacity for scholarly instruction. But Sir Thomas More, Chancellor of England from 1529 until his death in 1532, five years before Jane's birth, had swept such notions aside by providing a classical education for his own four daughters. He proved that girls could excel as easily as boys in such subjects. Lady Jane had showed an immediate aptitude for book work and with their aspirations firmly fixed on the child's future role, Frances and Henry Grey spared no pains to provide her with an education covering all branches of learning and etiquette that any future position in the royal household might demand.

Jane's first tutor was twenty-year-old John Aylmer[2], a Norfolk man and a Cambridge graduate, whom Henry Grey had sponsored during his Cambridge days. It was natural, therefore, that after graduating he should become resident chaplain at Bradgate for Henry Grey and his wife, with the education of the Grey girls as an obvious extension of this position. As we

have seen, the teachings of Scripture had won a strong foot-
hold in the English universities and John Aylmer was yet another Cambridge man caught up in this spiritual movement
which took its spring from the powerful impact of Scripture on
the mind and consciences of those who read and believed its
truths. The choice of such a man to be Jane Grey's first tutor
would have a profound effect on his pupil's entire life, and in it
we may clearly trace God's overruling purposes for the girl. From
the beginning Aylmer took the child to his heart. It is said that
for her earliest lessons he carried the diminutive girl around with
him and taught her the rudiments of reading and correct speech.
Jane responded to his interest and affection – having known
little enough of it in her short life so far.

From earliest days the Grey girls were trained in all the
protocol considered to be necessary in royal circles. And for Jane
in particular as the eldest daughter, the requirements and training
were stringent and demanding. The day would start at six in the
morning with a breakfast of bread, meat and ale, followed by
an inspection by her parents when they were at home. A strict
regime of lessons would occupy much of the day. Meals were
prolonged and elaborate and a correct code of behaviour expected from even the youngest child. Severe chastisement might
follow for the smallest deviation from the expected standards.

At the age of six this auburn-haired child, with a small freckled face and intelligent-looking brown eyes, began studying
Greek, Latin and modern languages. Dr Harding, another of
her father's chaplains and one who also gave every appearance
of upholding Reformation principles, was brought in to teach
her these subjects. Soon Jane was coping tolerably well with
simple translations from these other languages. At the same time
she was becoming proficient in reading her English Bible, much
of it translated by the martyred William Tyndale and now
licensed for circulation by the King. Hunting, hawking, dancing
and needlework were also part of her curriculum, as was music
at which Jane demonstrated clear talent.

For young Lady Jane, as for her parents, the overshadowing form of Henry VIII, with his enormous bulk and the power of life and death in his hand, dominated their home life. Nor was Jane allowed to forget her parents' ambitious hopes for her. Apart from her tutor John Aylmer, the girl's greatest friend and confidante during these first years of her life was her nurse, Mistress Ellen. Every day this kindly Scot would oversee the elaborate details of Jane's wardrobe. This was not an easy task for the girl would be dressed as a miniature adult: ornamental hoods set with jewels; wide-hooped skirts that prevented any small child from running or jumping; ornate bodices, intricately embroidered, complete with frilled ruffs at the wrists. With her petite form Jane must have presented a strange study in contrasts. At seven years of age the time was now approaching when the girl must be introduced to court life in London – scene of political intrigue, corruption and place-seeking which would form the backdrop for much of the rest of her life.

CHAPTER THREE

INTRODUCED TO COURT

L ady Frances Grey cared little for Jane, her eldest daughter. Strong-minded and determined, she saw the child merely as a tool with which to further her own ambition for power and prestige. Children had few enough rights in Tudor England and high-born girls were frequently regarded merely in terms of the advantage they could bring to their parents through an auspicious marriage. With a degree of satisfaction Jane's parents would have noted their child's outstanding intellectual capacity, for she soon gained a facility in Latin, Greek, French, Spanish and Italian, as well as in a study of the Scriptures. John Aylmer's careful instruction was clearly bearing fruit.

Rumours had also reached Leicestershire of Prince Edward's remarkable academic ability; and if Jane, this slightly-built bookish seven-year-old, had any prospect of being a future bride for the Prince, it was important that she too should reach a high standard in her studies. The possibility that Jane might one day be considered for this all-important role was gradually becoming more credible as news filtered through of Henry VIII's frustrations and diminishing hopes in his quest for a marriage contract for Edward with the Scottish child-queen, Mary Stuart. Henry had been vigorously pursuing this proposition since Mary's birth in 1542, when Edward and Jane were both four years of age; it was the more attractive because it would have brought with it an annexation of England's troublesome northern neighbour. But a ruthless military campaign in 1544 to enforce the alliance had left Edinburgh in flames and Holyrood Palace and Abbey ransacked. This had done little to endear the marriage proposal either to Mary's mother, the Scottish Queen Regent Mary of Guise, or to the Scottish nobility. In addition, the possibility had receded further when Scotland renewed its alliance with France

and another potential husband for the child Mary was born –
the Dauphin Francis, son of the future French king.

With royal blood in his veins and married to Henry VIII's
niece, Henry Grey, Marquess of Dorset, had been steadily
increasing both in wealth and status. Following the dissolution
of the monasteries some years earlier under Thomas Cromwell,
he had been prospered financially by the acquisition of a
further sixteen Leicestershire estates. Now he was among the
foremost members of the English nobility. Backed by his determined wife, only one thing still remained to promote his
ambitious designs: he must remind the King of the close
connection between the House of Tudor and the House of Grey.
Henry VIII, whose poor health suggested that he had not long
to live, must be made aware of his precocious great-niece.

In view of this, Jane's parents made arrangements to bring
their child to London to introduce her to court in 1544, soon
after her seventh birthday. In February of that same year Henry
VIII, realizing at last that he had no realistic hope of fathering
any more children, had presented Parliament with a new Act of
Succession, which allowed him to designate in his will who
should succeed to the throne in the event of his death. Obviously
Edward would be his heir, but should Edward die without
children, Henry stipulated that the throne would then pass to
Mary, his daughter by Katherine of Aragon, and if Mary had no
children, then to Elizabeth, Anne Boleyn's daughter. The
anomaly of this situation was the fact that both Mary and
Elizabeth had been declared illegitimate: the former upon his
marriage to Anne Boleyn, and the latter when Anne's execution
freed the King to marry Jane Seymour. According to the current
laws no person declared illegitimate could inherit the throne,
therefore in theory both Henry's daughters were disqualified
unless the Act were repealed – a thing that the King failed to do.
Finally, Henry specified that if all three of his children were to
die without heirs, the crown would pass, not to Frances Grey[1],
his younger sister's daughter, but to her children.[2] So by this
arrangement six-year-old Jane Grey became fourth in succession
to the throne.

Although we have no documentary evidence to colour in the details, it is interesting to imagine the first meeting between the royal cousins, Prince Edward and Lady Jane. Born in the same month, both were serious, highly intelligent children and both had been under the tuition of men who had embraced the biblical truths of the evangelical faith. Both had been taught to reverence the Scriptures and shared an aptitude and love of music. Needless to say, Henry and Frances Grey would hope that the fair-haired thoughtful Prince would form an early friendship with his cousin Jane.

The year before Jane's first visit to court, Henry had married yet again. As he recovered from his distress following the execution of Catherine Howard in 1542, he had begun looking around for some suitable candidate to take Catherine's place. To become Henry VIII's sixth wife was an unenviable prospect for any woman, and when the King's eyes rested on Katherine Parr she must have been filled with foreboding. Mature and attractive, she was also erudite to an exceptional measure among women of her generation and seemed well suited to occupy such an onerous position. But there was a problem: she was married. Coming from a long-established Westmoreland family Katherine had already been widowed once, and now, as the King must have observed with a degree of satisfaction, or perhaps relief, it did not seem likely that Katherine's second husband, the Lord Latimer, had long to live either. When an unsolicited gift from the King arrived for Katherine not long before her husband died, she must have guessed the hidden intent behind the gift.

Lord Latimer died on 2 March 1543, but at that very time another suitor appeared on the scene anxious to gain Katherine's hand: the ebullient and fickle Thomas Seymour, Prince Edward's uncle. Thomas Seymour had naturally risen to prominence, together with his older brother Edward, when their sister Jane Seymour had become Queen of England and had provided the King with his long-awaited heir. Handsome, seductive and charming in his manner, Thomas Seymour was always on the look-out for opportunities for self-aggrandizement. He too had noticed that Katherine would soon be widowed once more and had moved quickly to try to gain her affections for, despite her two previous marriages, Katherine was still only thirty and remained a beautiful woman.

Katherine, who was dutiful above all else, was strongly attracted to Thomas Seymour, and as she would later tell him, 'my mind was fully bent ... to marry you before any man I know'. But if the King of England required her hand she quickly decided to put aside all personal considerations and give herself in faithfulness to the ailing King. In July 1543 Henry made Katherine Parr his sixth wife – and a fine wife she proved to be. An early historian describes her 'great piety, beauty and discretion' and adds, 'next to the Bible, she studied the King's disposition'.[3] To be Henry VIII's sixth wife certainly called for one able to 'study the King's disposition'. His enormous bulk, his severely ulcerated leg that caused him incessant pain, and his erratic moods made him aggressive, moody and difficult. But Katherine remained gentle and considerate.

Fluent in several European languages and a fine conversationalist, Katherine was a tender-hearted woman, a fitting companion for Henry and a kindly stepmother to six-year-old Edward. Even Thomas Wriothesely, soon to become Lord Chancellor and no friend of the Reformation, grudgingly admitted, 'I am sure his Majesty never had a wife more agreeable to his heart than she is.' Katherine had an inner power that gave her strength for her precarious assignment as the wife of a King who could order his Queen's execution on the whim of a moment. From all contemporary records it is evident that she was a true Christian, a lover of God and of his Word. One of her chaplains could exclaim, 'Her rare goodness has made every day a Sunday, a thing hitherto unheard of, especially in a royal palace.'

Katherine acted both judiciously and patiently towards her husband yet was always seeking to influence him to promote the cause of true religion in his realm. She surrounded herself with ladies-in-waiting who shared her spiritual ideals. One of these was Catherine Brandon, the girl who as a fourteen-year-old had become fourth wife to Lady Jane's grandfather, Charles Brandon. Brandon, either from expediency or personal conviction, had been a firm supporter of the Reformation and Catherine too had fearlessly embraced those same evangelical truths. Full of spiritual zeal and love for God and his ways, she even had the audacity to call her pet spaniel 'Gardiner', a reference to Gardiner, Bishop of Winchester, who had worked so assiduously over the years to destroy the influence of the Reformation as well as its adherents.

Other women of devoted Christian character were gradually added to the Queen's inner circle, among them Anne Askew, who would later pay a high price for her faith. These high-born ladies spent time studying the Scriptures and praying together, and although Henry may well have known what was going on, he chose to ignore it. Through Katherine's influence evangelical preachers such as Hugh Latimer and Nicholas Ridley were invited to preach both at these private gatherings and before her at Hampton Court.

In Katherine Parr young Prince Edward had his first experience of the love of a mother; he quickly began to call her 'Mother'. Katherine's affection for the serious, fair-headed youngster was genuine, and in order to give him a taste of united family life she would frequently invite Mary, the King's elder daughter, to court; and at the same time she drew ten-year-old Elizabeth into the family circle. The two younger royal children took many of their lessons together and Katherine is usually credited with arranging for Sir John Cheke[4], Regius Professor of Greek at Cambridge and renowned English classicist, to join Dr Richard Cox as tutor to the Prince and his older sister. Sir John, another academic with strong evangelical persuasions, was also joined by Roger Ascham who would later take over Elizabeth's education. By these arrangements Katherine was ensuring that men of evangelical principle and commitment should influence Edward and Elizabeth at an important time in their lives. She also took a motherly interest in the Prince's progress and wrote to him when he was away studying at Greenwich Palace. It was probably at her suggestion that a group of other boys, sons of the gentry and nobility, joined Edward for lessons, giving the child a taste of more normal classroom life. Among these children were Catherine Brandon's sons, Henry and Charles, both serious minded and highly able boys.

Jane may well have formed an early attachment to Queen Katherine on this first visit to court in 1544, but two years later, by the time the girl was nine, it had become obvious to her parents that to keep Jane in the public eye she should not merely pay occasional visits to London but leave home and take up residence at court. If there were to be any hope of marrying Prince Edward she would need to learn the protocol and etiquette of court life. With this in mind Henry and Frances Grey made arrangements early in 1546 for Jane to exchange the quiet and beauty of Bradgate Park for a place among the maids-of-honour surrounding Queen Katherine at Hampton Court Palace.

Although much of Katherine's time was occupied with caring for the King, she kindly took the newcomer at court to her heart and gave Jane a degree of love and attention that she had never known before. Jane responded warmly to such concern and a close bond was forged between the Queen and the nine-year-old. For the first time in her short life Jane was treated with consideration and honour – a new experience for her.

Situated on the north bank of the River Thames, Hampton Court Palace was Henry VIII's favourite royal residence. Here his son Edward had been born and here, as the end of his life drew near, Henry spent much of his time. The gardens of Bradgate Manor paled to insignificance before the magnificent array of shrubs, ornamental trees, walkways, water features and fountains that surrounded Jane as she walked in these gardens. She would have been overawed at the splendour around her and yet relieved to be released from her mother's overbearing supervision.

Relationships between Jane and Prince Edward were seldom allowed to be anything but formal. Court etiquette demanded of Jane a degree of obeisance in the presence of her cousin that was most unnatural between two nine-year-olds. The children had much in common and the Prince would find that Jane was every bit his equal in the classroom – a salutary experience for him. During this happy interlude in her life, Jane now enjoyed the companionship of a number of other young people studying in the royal classroom. Lessons were most frequently conducted either in the healthier atmosphere of Enfield Palace – then in the heart of the country – or more usually at Greenwich Palace on the Thames. Thirteen-year-old Lady Elizabeth, although inclined to be a little remote and superior in her attitudes, was sometimes present. Prince Edward's special friend Barnaby Fitzpatrick, a likeable Irish boy of fourteen, was among his classmates. Another Edward, also fourteen and the Prince's cousin,[5] belonged to the group.

For one so young the Prince had made remarkable progress in his academic work. His Latin primer, which survives as well thumbed and grubby as that of any other schoolboy, bears witness to his endeavours. He could now write letters in Latin; and although a little stilted they were a token of his ability. Some of these were addressed to the father he wished he could see more often; some to Elizabeth to whom he wrote, 'There can be nothing pleasanter than a letter from you … it is some comfort that I might hope to visit you soon if nothing happens to either of us in the meantime'. He would write to his older sister, Mary, of whom he seemed particularly fond, but most frequently his letters were addressed to his stepmother, Katherine Parr, who took a warm interest in all his activities.

Like any other boy, however, the Prince could become both bored and disinclined to do his work. It is recorded that on occasions his tutor, Sir John Cheke, dealt some well-deserved blows to the royal bottom after repeated warnings had been given. More often, as Edward grew older, Barnaby Fitzpatrick was his 'whipping-boy'. When the Prince merited chastisement,

Barnaby was obliged to stand in for him – though doubtless Edward was expected to watch the proceedings.

Edward was surrounded by men of strong spiritual convictions. It was a privilege for him to listen to sermons from some of the most earnest evangelical preachers in the land, men of the calibre of Nicholas Ridley and Hugh Latimer. Edward early became persuaded of the truths of Scripture and there is evidence from his written work, still existing, of his strong personal commitment to those truths. He was aware that his sister Mary held tenaciously to Catholic doctrine but in his own childish way he hoped and looked for her conversion to the faith he had embraced.

Nine-year-old Jane, meanwhile, had settled in among the Queen's ladies-in-waiting although much of her time was taken up with her education. Whenever she was able we can well imagine that Jane Grey would join a number of others who, like Katherine herself, were sincere Christians gathering together regularly to study the Scriptures. Whatever ulterior motives her parents may have had for placing Jane in the royal court at this time, a divine purpose transcended any human arrangements. During this period of her life the teachings of the Bible, carefully inculcated by John Aylmer, became regenerating truth in the child's heart. Forgiveness of sin and acceptance with God, not through any acts of merit on the part of the sinner, but through the grace and mercy of God in Christ, became a felt experience for Jane as she found in the Son of God both a Saviour and friend. Now prayer was no mere formality but a path to personal communion with God.

Historians, with little understanding of true heart-religion, and with an accompanying measure of prejudice against any for whom faith in God is an all-consuming dedication, use such words as 'fanatical' and 'extreme' when they speak of the religious zeal of Lady Jane and of Prince Edward. The truth remains that these children had been caught up in an astonishing work of God, loosely called the Reformation – one that brought spiritual renewal to generations of men and women and which would affect the whole course of world history.

Bradgate Park. The manor house, where once Jane enjoyed peace and quiet, is now a ruin.

CHAPTER FOUR

THE SHADOW OF DEATH

As the end of Henry VIII's life drew ever closer, his physical agony intensified and with it his moods grew yet more erratic. Although he had dismissed some of the Roman Catholic dogma, with the power of the papacy as its centralizing point, Henry had no alternative focus for his faith. He had severed himself and his country from papal jurisdiction, and had therefore forfeited the pope's supposed powers to mitigate the pains of purgatory. Still rejecting the evangelical doctrine of justification by faith, and now in the face of his own impending death, he knew no other way by which guilt could be removed.

Since the collapse of the Catherine Howard marriage and his marriage to Katherine Parr, the Reforming party had been in favour. There had been few executions or burnings of so-called 'heretics' – men and women who read and loved the Scriptures – since 1543. But without any secure anchor for his soul and still nominally adhering to much Catholic teaching, Henry's favours now began to veer back in that direction. Politically also, as we have seen, he had long vacillated between the Catholic faction and the Evangelicals, preferring which ever best served his interests. The death, in 1545, of Charles Brandon, Lady Jane's grandfather and Henry VIII's brother-in-law, was a further significant factor for it had taken from the King one of the staunchest supporters of the Reformation.

Men such as Stephen Gardiner, the Bishop of Winchester, and Thomas Wriothesley, the Lord Chancellor, were quick to note the fluctuation in the King's patronage. Since 1543, with the support of the Queen, the Evangelicals had grown ever more bold and the fact that the heir to the throne was now being tutored by men of this persuasion was a source of consternation to these supporters of Catholic tradition. Active over the years in trying to suppress the influence of Reformation teaching in England, Gardiner and Wriothesley began to seek further opportunities to arrest its advance. They well knew that the Archbishop, Thomas Cranmer, was among the foremost in advancing a programme of church reform, of removing images from church buildings and impeding, wherever possible, those clergy who promoted the 'Old Religion' from holding positions of influence. But despite a concerted effort to blacken the Archbishop in Henry's eyes during 1543, they failed, for the King had a deep personal attachment to Cranmer and was unwilling to lose his Archbishop.

Instead Gardiner and his co-workers contented themselves with more vulnerable prey: four men living in the Oxford area were arraigned, accused and burnt in 1544 for no greater cause than their refusal to worship images and relics and to desist from reading the Scriptures. Unable to undermine and remove Cranmer from office, these ardent Catholics, together with such men as Edmund Bonner, Bishop of London, were undeterred. They would aim yet higher. The Queen herself was surely foremost in encouraging the spread of biblical truth, initially in the court, and then through evangelical preachers to the people.

Not daring to strike at the throne directly they found an easier target: Anne Askew, bright, articulate and fearless, was a lady-in-waiting to the Queen. Had she not been diligently promoting the spread of evangelical literature among the London apprentice boys? She had even been heard to say 'I would sooner read five lines in the Bible than hear five masses in the church.' Such words were heresy in Catholic eyes. Anne was seized, imprisoned and interrogated cruelly by Bonner. She was subjected to torture and then, when no word of concession nor any betrayal of the Queen and others in the royal circle could be wrung from the suffering woman, condemned to death. Anne prayed earnestly for her persecutors: 'Lord, let them never overcome me with vain words, but fight thou, Lord, in my stead, for on thee I cast my care... Lord, I heartily desire of thee that thou wilt of thy merciful goodness forgive them that violence which they do and have done unto me. Open also thou their blind hearts...'[1]

Declaring 'I would sooner die than break my faith,' Anne Askew was burnt at Smithfield as a heretic on 16 July 1546.

With Anne's death, young Jane Grey, who was at Hampton Court throughout this period, witnessed at first hand the price a young woman was prepared to pay for holding fast to the truth of Scripture and particularly the cost of maintaining that the bread, consecrated in the Mass, did not become the actual physical body of Christ. Many more Christian men and women would die rather than accept this dogma, and having seen Anne's courage, it would become a conviction that Jane too carried in her heart as an unshakeable belief.

Following this martyrdom, a success for the Traditionalists, plans were carefully laid to ensnare the Queen herself. Lies, insinuation, scurrilous suggestions: these were the tools with which they tried to undermine Katherine's credibility with the King. Playing on his inordinate pride and the superiority he assumed as Head of the Church, Wriothesley and Gardiner endeavoured to persuade Henry that his wife was far too outspoken in her religious views. Worse than this, she was even prepared to lecture him in front of his courtiers. At first the King's true affection for Katherine made their efforts fruitless. Still they waited their moment to strike, using the intervening time to draw up an indictment against the Queen. In it they would accuse her of violating Henry's orders by reading prohibited books; of openly propagating heretical doctrines and of undermining the *Six Articles*, drawn up in 1539, that set out basic Catholic teaching concerning the Mass. All they needed now was the right occasion to stir up the King's anger against Katherine to a sufficient degree, making him willing to entertain their accusations and to sign the indictment. Then the Queen would be in their power. The Evangelical party would soon crumble.

As Henry's weakness increased and the pain from his ulcerated leg grew worse, he became yet more morose and unpredictable and was mainly confined to his private apartments at his palace at Whitehall. Then came their opportunity: his two statesmen were present with the King on one occasion when

Katherine, troubled about the King's spiritual state, addressed him a little too freely concerning his need to find mercy through Christ alone. Henry clearly did not appreciate being spoken to like that in the presence of members of his Privy Council, and by a mere woman as well. His face darkened and he changed the subject. But Gardiner and Wriothesley had noticed. After Katherine had retired from the King's presence and he was alone with his statesmen, they once more took the opportunity to vilify the Queen and then presented the indictment: in a weak moment Henry was prevailed upon to sign a warrant for Katherine's arrest. So near to the grave himself he was still prepared to allow yet another wife to follow two previous ones to the execution block.

Then an extraordinary thing happened. As Wriothesley left the King he carelessly dropped the signed indictment. One of the palace staff picked it up and, realizing its sensitive nature, hurried to show it to the Queen. The shock of what she read, signed by Henry himself, threw Katherine into a state of hysterical weeping. Death loomed before her, and not for her only but for those who shared her faith. When news of the Queen's distress reached Henry, whose conscience had been troubling him in any case, he ordered that he should be carried across to the Queen's apartments. The sight of Katherine's swollen, tear-stained face and her terror was enough for Henry to put aside his annoyance and try to comfort his wife with reassurances of his affection.

A nine-year-old child had been the silent witness of this unfolding scenario. Jane Grey's own distress at the dangers surrounding the one whom she had loved like a mother is not hard to imagine. Still unsure of Henry's attitude, Katherine could not rest content until she had made a full confession of all her perceived faults to the King. The next evening she crossed to Whitehall Palace, taking just two companions with her. One was her sister, and some early accounts of this unhappy episode suggest that the other one may have been Jane.[2] Reaching the King's apartment, Katherine threw herself down in front of him and begged his pardon for overstepping her prerogatives as a woman. She flattered, she cajoled, she undertook to submit herself to him as her superior both by nature and position and to learn wisdom from her husband in future. She knew that only a mere change of mood stood between her and the executioner's axe. 'And is it even so, sweet heart?' said Henry kindly, kissing his wife. 'Then perfect friends are we now again.'

Only the next day, as Katherine and several of her ladies-in-waiting were speaking to the King, forty shiny halberds, axe-heads fixed to long shafts, were seen gleaming in the sun through the surrounding trees. It was Wriothesley, unaware that his plans had gone awry, come with forty soldiers to arrest the Queen. Astonished to find the King apparently reconciled to his Queen, he scarcely knew what to say. But when the King spoke to him in a low whisper, and then in a louder voice declared, 'Fool, beast, arrant knave, be gone!' he had little doubt that he had been foiled in his endeavour. It was a reversal of circumstance that Lady Jane would not easily forget.

Not only had the Catholic party failed to gain its highest prize, the repercussions of this whole affair were the reverse of their intentions. Both Stephen Gardiner and Thomas Wriothesley, chief perpetrators in this failed endeavour, saw their position and influence eclipsed. The Evangelical party rose to favour once more. Knowing that his own days were numbered, Henry was anxious to leave the kingdom secure for his son. He feared the intentions of the Catholic party and particularly perceived the flamboyant and intelligent Henry Howard, Earl of Surrey and son of the ageing Duke of Norfolk, as a threat. So when Henry Howard had the indiscretion to remember that he was descended from Edward I (from whom the family traced their claim to the throne) and to embody the arms of Edward the Confessor on his family crest, it was interpreted as a declaration of his aspiration to the crown. Rumour added a spicy accusation: this dashing young nobleman and poet hoped to seek the hand of the Lady Mary in marriage, a move that could endanger Prince Edward's claim to the throne. The King acted

swiftly: the young man was arrested, accused of an act of treason and executed forthwith.

Thomas Howard, elderly father of Henry Howard, had been
a life-long supporter of the 'Old Religion', and remained among
the most powerful men in the land. Ten years earlier Howard
had been one of the perpetrators of the accusations that had
led to the death of Anne Boleyn, and had more recently taken a
prominent part in the torture and death of Anne Askew. Despite
his age and long record of service to the crown, Thomas Howard
too was put in prison to await execution. With the Catholic
party now seriously weakened, Henry ensured that the interests of the men who surrounded his son would be best served
by supporting the Reforming party. The Prince's uncles, the
Seymour brothers – Edward and Thomas – were placed in
positions of influence within the Privy Council. In this way Henry
VIII aimed to secure a stable future for Prince Edward.

But soon this despotic monarch, who could sign death
warrants with ease, had himself to appear before the Judge of
all. By January 1547 he was seriously ill. No one dared tell the
King that he was dying, but at last, seeing that his strength was
fast declining, one of his noblemen urged Henry to prepare for
death as nothing more could be done for him. It has been said
that the despotic old King grieved over his sins on his deathbed,
and even regretted his offence against Anne Boleyn, but this
cannot be verified. At last, too weak to speak, Henry indicated
that he would like to see his Archbishop, Thomas Cranmer.
'Give me some token with your eyes or hand that you trust in
the Lord,' said Cranmer. Wringing the Archbishop's hand with
all the strength he could muster, Henry VIII at last laid down the
reins of power. A nine-year-old boy would succeed him on the
throne of England.

CHAPTER FIVE
UP FOR SALE

Prince Edward and his sister the Lady Elizabeth were together at Enfield Palace when told of their father's death. Both dissolved into broken-hearted weeping and clung to each other. Although Henry could abuse others and cruelly renege on his expressions of friendship, his children, despite his treatment of Elizabeth who had been declared illegitimate after the execution of her mother, had held him in high respect. Edward had been trained to think of his father as a model of kingship that he must strive to emulate. Edward Seymour, the prince's older uncle who had broken the news to the children, decided to leave the boy where he was for the rest of the day, before escorting him to the Tower of London the following day. Here, according to custom, he would wait for three weeks before his coronation.

Henry had left instructions for a regency comprised of sixteen men to be established at his death to govern the country until Edward reached his majority. But the old King had scarcely been dead two days before his plans were overturned. Edward Seymour had hurried straight from Henry's deathbed to Enfield Palace, told the boy of his father's death, and then assumed custody of his nephew. Cleverly managed, it now placed Seymour in an unassailable position to take over the reins of power himself. Instead of a regency, therefore, the Council had little option other than to agree that there should be a protectorate. Edward Seymour had none to stand in his way or to prevent him from becoming Lord Protector – a circumstance that aroused considerable jealousy among the other members of the Council and sowed the seeds of a bitter harvest for the nobleman. Even though the new king was assured that he would be given all the respect enjoyed by his father and be informed of the decisions undertaken on his behalf, the fact remained that the nation would be ruled with little reference to him.

Three weeks of preparations for the coronation ensued, a two-day event that would be the most momentous in Edward's nine years. But before that took place he performed one of his first public functions – one that would colour his entire future more than he could know. He agreed, together with the Council, that his uncle Edward Seymour should be Lord Protector, and also conferred on him the title of Duke of Somerset. Edward's other uncle, Thomas Seymour, would now become the Lord Admiral, while John Dudley, who currently held that position, was given an earldom becoming Earl of Warwick. These three men were to play major roles in the remaining years of Edward's life. All nominally supported the Reforming or Evangelical party, at least while it was propitious to do so.

With a riot of pomp, splendour and colour, Edward left the Tower on 19 February 1547 for the first stage of his coronation, called the Accession. Seated on a horse which was ornately clad in crimson and decorated with diamonds, the child was dressed in a contrasting silver gown with gold embroidery and a belt of silver, glistening with rubies and diamonds. His white velvet cap was studded with jewels. With grandees riding to left and right of him and Lady Jane's father, Henry Grey, carrying the Sword of State before him, the procession set off. The streets were lined with cheering, singing crowds, many gaining their first sight of their new King. Edward had been well trained and behaved impeccably, but it must have been a weary boy who slept that night in the Palace of Westminster.

The coronation itself took place the following day. For this more private ceremony Edward was arrayed in crimson velvet embroidered with gold and wore a black velvet cap. A serious boy, Edward listened with close attention to the admonitions and charges made to him by his godfather, Archbishop Thomas Cranmer. He understood that his spiritual duty was to care for the souls of his people, to reign wisely and justly – a heavy burden for his nine-year-old shoulders to carry. 'You are to reward virtue, to revenge sin, to justify the innocent, to relieve the poor, to procure peace, to repress violence, and to execute justice throughout your realms,' Cranmer charged the nine-year-old. Three separate crowns were used during the ceremony: the crown of St Edward and the Crown Imperial, together with a small replica of the Crown Imperial especially made to fit the child's head.

Following the concluding prayer, the young King, now solemnly proclaimed Supreme Head of the Church, left the Abbey and led the way to Westminster Hall where the coronation banquet was to be held. An anecdote has survived which gives clear evidence of the seriousness with which he viewed his new responsibilities. Carried before him in stately symbolism were three swords. Surprised, Edward stopped the procession and asked for an explanation. He was told that each was to represent one part of his kingdom: England, Ireland and France. 'One is wanting', was his unexpected reply, 'the Bible. That book is the sword of the Spirit and to be preferred before these swords.' Quickly the Bible was removed from the lectern and at his insistence carried in front of the three swords representing his temporal kingdom.[1]

The death of Henry VIII and the accession and coronation of Edward marked dramatic changes in the lives of many others besides the young King. The first to feel the change was Katherine Parr, Henry's widow. No provision had been made in the late King's will for her to have any continuing role in the life of her stepson, even though in her position as Queen dowager she retained precedence over the King's daughters. She must immediately move out of Whitehall Palace and take up residence at her own home, Chelsea Manor. Confiscated from the estates of Sir Thomas More in 1530, Chelsea Manor had been given to Katherine by Henry VIII as her personal possession. An attractive brick-built mansion, it stood on the site of present-day Cheyne Walk. Katherine took thirteen-year-old Elizabeth with her; the princess would live with her stepmother until her education was complete. But for nine-year-old Lady Jane Grey there was no alternative but to return home to Bradgate, in Leicestershire.

Another whose position would alter significantly was the new Lord Admiral, Thomas Seymour, younger brother of Edward Seymour, the Protector. His dashing demeanour, charm and effusive manner hid a jealous and intense ambition. He strongly resented his brother's superior position and purposed to do all he could to undermine it. His first plan was to make an advantageous marriage for himself. He tried to win the hand of three ladies in succession: Anne of Cleves, Henry's rejected fourth wife; Lady Mary, now in her early thirties, and even Elizabeth, only thirteen. When all these propositions failed, he made a daring bid for the hand of Katherine Parr herself. Here he was in a more hopeful position for he knew well that she had loved him sincerely before she married Henry. He had even received a recent letter from Katherine in which she reminded him of her love, before, as she expressed it, 'God called upon me to renounce utterly mine own will' and marry Henry instead. Now free once more she hinted that her affections for the Admiral remained unchanged.

Thomas Seymour's problem lay not in winning Katherine's heart but in the public outcry that might be caused if he married Henry's widow so soon after the King's death. The only way to circumvent such a reaction was to obtain the new King's acquiescence in the plan; then neither the Privy Council nor his older brother Edward could easily object. Success was not too difficult to achieve for a nine-year-old can be easily persuaded, especially when the required favours come hidden under the cloak of extra pocket money and small gifts. Katherine and Thomas Seymour were married privately shortly afterwards and soon moved away together from Chelsea Manor to the quiet location of Hanworth, another of Katherine's palaces bequeathed to her by Henry VIII, not far from present-day Heathrow Airport.

With a wife whose prestige would enhance his own, for Katherine still held the rank of first Lady in the land, the Lord Admiral began to plan the next stage of his political advance. His mind turned to Lady Jane Grey. He knew well that his older brother, the Protector, was set on pursuing Henry VIII's plan for Edward to gain a marriage contract with young Mary Stuart the Scottish queen; in fact a further military campaign against Scotland was being planned at that very time. But in the event of the failure of that scheme, which seemed increasingly likely, the Protector had made tentative plans to marry his own daughter to the King.

The Protector also had plans for Jane. He hoped to marry her to his fourteen-year-old son, also named Edward, the boy who had studied with Jane in the royal schoolroom. Although Thomas Seymour knew that Jane's parents, Henry and Frances Grey, had entertained this last proposition favourably, he began to consider setting before them a yet more glittering prize. His purpose was twofold: by reviving their hopes of a marriage settlement for Jane with the King himself, he might also be able to bribe the Greys into compliance with his other underhand schemes to gain the ultimate power he coveted.

It was well known that King Edward was very fond of Jane and that she was in every way his equal intellectually, but court etiquette prevented any relaxed friendship between the Tudor cousins. Jane was expected to curtsey three times as she approached the boy, kneel when he addressed her, and wait for permission to sit on a cushion at his feet. At the end of a game or conversation together she must kiss his hand and leave the room, walking backwards. Despite all this most unhelpful protocol, sixteenth-century documents record that Jane was 'most dear unto the king, both in regard to religion and of her knowledge' – an indication of Jane's early piety as well as of her intelligence.

Henry and Frances Grey, whose own future eminence was tied up with Jane's marriage settlement, had also been carefully watching all the proceedings at the royal palaces, with its internal power struggles. So when the Admiral, Thomas Seymour, approached them, he had little difficulty in gaining their compliance with his suggestions of that grandiose prospect for their daughter that they had dreamed of since Jane's birth. Understandably

Jane's parents now waited eagerly to see if the Admiral would take steps to carry out his alleged intentions. When the ambitious father could curb his patience no longer, he tried to contact the Admiral to discuss his plans for Jane. Unable to speak in person to Henry Grey at the time, Thomas Seymour sent him a message urging patience and restraint, reassuring him that he had indeed important schemes afoot for Jane. He hinted yet again that marriage to the King was certainly a distinct possibility.

Thomas Seymour then attempted to execute his plan. First he continued to curry favour with Edward by giving him extra pocket money (it was to his advantage that the boy's other uncle was parsimonious and over-strict with his nephew), and then he gradually sowed the thought of a marriage with Lady Jane into the King's mind. Although Edward was fond of Jane, his dedication to his father's ambitions that he should marry Mary Stuart weighed strongly with him, and even if this proved impossible, he dreamed of a more propitious arrangement than marriage to his quiet, auburn-haired cousin. Perhaps some wealthy Continental princess might be available. He was therefore not prepared to entertain his uncle's suggestions. But when Edward's tutor, Sir John Cheke, discovered extra pocket money in his pupil's possession, he asked the boy about it. Edward confessed that it was a gift from his Uncle Thomas and also disclosed the marriage suggestion. Cheke immediately reported this to the Protector, whose fury with his brother's furtive schemes can well be imagined.

Meanwhile Henry and Frances Grey continued to wait, still receiving no assurance of any progress in Jane's affairs. Nor did they know of the setback the Admiral had experienced, or that he had decided to let the whole matter drop for the present. At last Henry Grey, no doubt urged on by his ambitious wife, arrived at Seymour Place, the Admiral's official London home, and demanded to speak to him in private. Carefully taking the anxious father out of earshot of the servants, Thomas Seymour made a staggering offer. If Henry Grey would sell Jane and all her marriage rights to him, he would pay liberally. With a mixture of flattery and bribery he continued, 'Lady Jane is as handsome a lady [she was not quite ten years of age] as any in England, and she might be wife to any prince in Christendom.' He continued with a further vague hint of a possible marriage to the King and offered her father £2000 for Jane. Making a large down payment of £500, he concluded the deal and the child officially passed into his guardianship. Henry Grey had sold his responsibility for the welfare and future of his own daughter for personal advantage.

Early in May 1547 Jane, accompanied by her nurse Mistress Ellen and one or two other personal attendants, left Bradgate once more, this time to live at Hanworth Palace as the ward of Thomas Seymour and Katherine. Whether Jane knew of the financial deal that lay behind this sudden change in her circumstances is uncertain, but it is unlikely that she shed many tears over leaving her parent's home. She admired the Admiral, not as yet seeing through his duplicity and, as we have seen, had a close bond with Lady Katherine. Elizabeth was also there and the two girls continued to study together, although with a four-year age gap, there is little evidence of a strong friendship developing between them. Miles Coverdale, who had assisted William Tyndale in his translation work of part of the Old Testament, and had been responsible for seeing the first complete English Bible through the press in 1535, had returned to England following Henry's death. He now acted as Katherine's personal chaplain and tutor to both the girls.

Although King Edward was far from content at the way his older uncle, the Lord Protector, was taking the prerogatives of kingship to himself, making decisions without consulting him and keeping him short of pocket money, he had begun to see that his younger uncle had been ingratiating himself into his favour in order to further his own schemes. Day by day Thomas Seymour had been sowing critical thoughts in the boy's mind regarding the Protector, and appearing to make himself the champion of Edward's cause. But Edward was astute enough to suspect his younger uncle's motives and was growing ever more wary of him. The relationship between the Seymour brothers had deteriorated yet further when it became evident that Thomas was unwilling to do his duties as Lord Admiral – duties that would have taken him overseas, away from the seat of power and the scenes of his clandestine operations.

Another who was secretly plotting the overthrow of the Protector was the second most powerful man in the Kingdom, John Dudley, whom Edward VI had created Earl of Warwick shortly before his coronation. He was more subtle and clever than the Admiral and was content to watch and wait to see if Thomas Seymour would destroy his brother or be destroyed by him. Either way it could turn to Dudley's own advantage. Among the men who held the reins of power, only Thomas Cranmer appeared a genuine friend to the King.

In the early winter of 1547 Jane Grey was pleased to learn that her much loved friend and protector, Katherine, was expecting her first child. Although this was her fourth marriage, and she was already thirty-five years of age, like everyone else at Hanworth Katherine was delighted at the prospect. Only one thing marred her joy: her husband's ill-concealed friendship with Lady Elizabeth – not long turned fourteen.

At first it took the form of playful romps and showmanship in the presence of the adolescent princess. Then it grew more serious as Thomas repeatedly entered Elizabeth's bedroom before she was dressed in the morning and cavorted around the bed, teasing the girl. The apparent fun was becoming distinctly alarming as Elizabeth, not surprisingly, appeared to enjoy the attention. But when Katherine discovered her husband and the young Elizabeth locked in one another's arms, she knew she must act and quickly. Elizabeth's own mother, Anne Boleyn, had died for suspected infidelities trumped up by her enemies. What would happen to Elizabeth if this conduct were discovered? Without hesitation she sent the girl away to stay with friends in Cheshunt, ensuring that there was no further contact between her husband and Elizabeth. Only the discretion and prompt action on Katherine's part protected Elizabeth – who had scarcely

realized the possible consequences of the liberties she had
allowed to Thomas Seymour.

As the date for Katherine's confinement drew closer she and
Lady Jane left Hanworth, together with the usual royal retinue
and Katherine's chaplain, Miles Coverdale, bound for Sudeley
Castle – another of the Seymour estates. Not far from the quiet
Gloucestershire village of Winchcombe, Sudeley was a peace-
ful spot, surrounded by woodland and set in the heart of the
Cotswolds. The stately home, with its many shapely yew trees,
formal gardens and walkways, may well have reminded Jane of
her own family home in Leicestershire. But the days spent at
Sudeley were not happy ones for either Katherine or Jane. Since
Katherine's intervention to prevent Lady Elizabeth facing
public disgrace, any semblance of affection that the Admiral,
Thomas Seymour, might have shown his wife had gone. He
seldom visited her and many of his movements seemed shrouded
in mystery. Before Henry's death Katherine had been spending
her spare moments writing a book, the title of which was *A Lamentation or Complaint of a Sinner.* [2] Perhaps she picked up the
manuscript again at this period prior to her confinement and
decided that it was now safe to publish it. It is a book that records
the path this earnest evangelical queen had taken as she came
to a true understanding of justification by faith; its pages may
also have brought fresh spiritual consolation to Katherine as she
grieved over her husband's evident rejection of her. In her book
she recalled the days when she had once spurned the tender
mercy and grace of God:

> Oh, how miserably and wretchedly am I confounded when
> for the multitude and greatness of my sins, I am com-
> pelled to accuse myself! Was it not a marvellous
> unkindness, when God did speak to me and also call to
> me, that I would not answer him?…What a wretch am I
> that when the Prince of princes, the King of Kings did
> speak many pleasant and gentle words unto me and also
> called me by so many sundry times, yet notwithstanding

these great signs and tokens of love I would not come unto him.

She continued to grieve over her unbelief and hardness of heart, until she realized that there was hope for desolate sinners:

What! Shall I fall into desperation? Nay, I will call upon Christ, the Light of the world; the Fountain of life, the relief of all careful consciences, the peacemaker between God and man, and the only comfort of all repentant sinners.

We can follow her gradual enlightenment until at last Katherine could declare: 'Many will wonder and marvel at this my saying, that I never knew Christ for my Saviour and Redeemer until this time.'[3] She had discovered that despite all the tradition in which she had been schooled it was 'by faith only I am sure to be justified', and could now rejoice in 'an earnest love to the truth inspired by God who promiseth to pour his Spirit upon all flesh; which I have by the grace of God'. The book was a remarkable work for a sixteenth-century woman, and has additional poignancy in view of Katherine's brave stand for truth and the neglect she was experiencing from Thomas Seymour.

On 30 August 1548 a baby daughter named Mary was born to Katherine at Sudeley Castle. Thomas had arrived in time for the confinement and sent a letter to his brother in London to tell of the infant's birth. But the celebrations were short-lived because it soon became evident that Katherine had succumbed to puerperal sepsis or child-bed fever as it was called. In her delirium Katherine was heard to whisper, 'I am not well-handled, for those that be about me care not for me, but stand laughing at my grief.' In the hearing of her husband she continued, 'the more good I will to them, the less good they will do to me.' 'Why, sweet heart', expostulated the Admiral in a jocular tone, 'I would do you no hurt.' But Katherine knew better. 'No, my lord,' she replied, 'I think so.' But despite the way he had treated her, when she made her will she left all her considerable possessions to the unworthy Admiral for she had truly loved him. 'I wish I had a thousand times as much to leave him,' was her pathetic comment. Eight days after Mary's birth her mother died, leaving behind the infant daughter who lived for about a year, cared for by relatives. Lady Jane Grey had lost her truest friend.

The Admiral did not stay at Sudeley for the funeral but hastened to London to tell Edward of the death of his stepmother. Edward sent instructions that the funeral was to be conducted with all the ceremony of a royal occasion, for was she not the widow of Henry VIII? Heralds, ushers, six bearers in hooded gowns, candle bearers... it was to be an impressive affair, but on the occasion there was only one official mourner. A small lonely figure of a girl, not yet eleven years of age and wearing a long black dress with a velvet purple train, followed the coffin. Jane was followed by members of the household walking in pairs. The service in the chapel which adjoins the Castle was conducted in simple Protestant style by Miles Coverdale, soon to become one of Edward's chaplains and Bishop of Exeter. Katherine had been among the noblest women of the Reformation and her loss was a grievous one for Lady Jane Grey.

CHAPTER SIX

PLOTS... PLOTS... PLOTS

Following the death of Katherine there seemed little reason for Lady Jane Grey to remain at Sudeley Castle. Soon the Marquess of Dorset and his wife notified Thomas Seymour that they wished to have their child back at Bradgate Manor. Their letter requesting Jane's return is sufficiently deferential to Seymour to demonstrate that the money paid out for the girl gave him the final word over her arrangements. 'My good brother,' wrote Frances, 'my request shall be that I may have the oversight of her with your good will and thereby I shall have good reason to think that you do trust me...' Reluctantly Seymour agreed, for at that moment he was clearly in no position to make adequate provision for his young ward. However, when Jane returned, her parents were not well pleased with the change they noticed in their daughter. She had turned eleven in that month, October 1548, but was old for her years; and the experiences she had lived through had matured her – experiences that few children of her age had faced.

At court Jane had been shown deference and honour in her present position as third in line for the throne. She had been a constant companion to Katherine and, with her favoured status in the young King's friendship, had enjoyed privileges and respect. All this would disappear on her return home. Her parents also soon discovered that Jane had developed clear opinions of her own and was prepared to articulate them, making her less than submissive to their every wish. Added to this, there was another change that would not have escaped their notice. Those biblical truths that Jane had first learnt at home from her tutor, John Aylmer, had now become her personal spiritual convictions. Henry and Frances Grey also supported the 'New Religion' and her father had corresponded with some of the Swiss Reformers, but their commitment was nominal at best.

In Jane they discovered a heart reliance on the truths of Scripture: her outlook, interests and reactions had radically altered.

From Jane's point of view she would have been glad to see her younger sisters again. Nine-year-old Katherine, already a beautiful child, was a favourite with her parents and more compliant with their wishes than Jane; Mary her small hump-backed sister was now five. The peace of the woods of Bradgate with their autumn shades of reds and golds, the bronze of the bracken clothing the surrounding hills, the deer bounding freely among the rocky outcrops, must have afforded a measure of relief to the child after her solitary role at the death and funeral of her closest friend, Katherine Parr.

But her parents' attitude to their daughter grew steadily more disagreeable as the days passed. In their view she had been spoilt by the attention she had received – and here they may well have been right. Her intellectual ability had earned praise, even adulation from all about her. Now she received little else apart from rebukes and criticism. Even harder for Jane to bear was the fact that she represented failure in her parents' eyes. Thomas Seymour had not succeeded in gaining a marriage alliance with Edward, or with 'any [other] prince in Christendom' as he had promised. The Greys' own dreams of grandeur and advancement were looking far more fanciful.

Not many weeks had elapsed before Seymour, recovering from the shock of Katherine's death, realized his folly in permitting Jane to return home. Paying a personal visit to her father at his London home, Dorset Place in Westminster, he urged him with all the persuasiveness and charm of his usual bearing to allow the girl to come back to him. Lady Frances was far from ready to grant her permission. She was concerned about who would care for Jane if she returned; for this the Admiral had a ready answer. He had decided to retain all his late wife's maids-of-honour and, in addition, his own mother Lady Seymour had agreed to come and take charge of the household. She would keep a motherly eye on Jane, he assured Frances, and added, 'For my own part I will be a half-father, and more.' How could they wish for a better arrangement? He continued that he had decided not to arrange a marriage alliance for Jane at present but would wait until she had reached child-bearing age.

Such a veiled comment could have several interpretations. Clearly it meant that he was in no hurry to promote a contract for Jane with the King but a further interpretation was being spread in whispers around the corridors of the royal palaces: the ambitious Admiral was thinking of marrying her himself. 'There hath been a tale of late', he is reported to have confided to one of Elizabeth's courtiers, 'they say now I shall marry my Lady Jane. I tell you this but merrily – merrily.' How merrily we cannot now know.

Disgruntled at the lack of any obvious resolution of plans for Jane's future, Frances Grey was still not satisfied with Seymour's plausible suggestions and said she was unwilling to allow Jane to rejoin his household. Henry Grey wrote to the Admiral voicing concerns about their daughter who, in their view, could 'hardly rule herself as yet without a guide'. They told Seymour that they feared lest Jane should 'for lack of a bridle take too much the head, and conceive such opinion of herself that all such good behaviour as she hath heretofore learned by the Queen's and your most wholesome instructions, should either altogether be quenched in her, or at least much diminished'. Quite clearly they felt that Jane needed a heavy hand upon her to prevent her from becoming too opinionated, and so continued, 'I shall in most hearty wise require your lordship to commit her to the governance of her mother, by whom, for the fear and duty she oweth her, she [Jane] shall be most easily ruled and framed unto virtue.' In order for this to be accomplished Henry Grey was sure that 'the eye and oversight of my wife shall be in this respect most necessary'. Her mother would be in a better position to ensure that the girl began 'addressing her mind to humility, soberness, and obedience'.[1] The strength of character which was to become so marked a feature of Lady Jane in the future was already in evidence and her parents did not like it.

Hidden beneath their excuses was another reason for Henry and Frances Grey's unwillingness to allow Jane to return to Seymour Place. In spite of having accepted money for Jane's marriage rights, her parents had been secretly reviving a previous marriage proposal for their girl. Despairing of ever seeing her married to the King, they had returned to their former proposition as the next best option: that she should marry Edward Seymour, fourteen-year-old son of the Protector. Jane was well acquainted with the young man from her lessons with the King and his fellow pupils, and there is every likelihood that the proposal appealed to her.

The weeks passed and the Admiral's plans for undermining his brother, the Protector, and for placing himself in the position of supreme power in the Council, were now maturing. He needed Jane in his charge, for her presence at his court formed an integral part of his strategy. Jane, too, was increasingly unhappy at home and letters that she wrote to the Admiral hint, in the circuitous style of the day, that she wished to be under his roof again. Once more Seymour approached the Marquess and his wife to repeat his request that they allow Jane to join him. But it was only after renewed pledges that he would attempt to marry her to Edward VI, and the sight of a further £500 of the money which he had agreed to pay for Jane's marriage rights, that he at last gained his wish. Once more Lady Jane was returned to the care of Thomas Seymour. More than this, the transfer of money meant that Jane's parents now had a vested interest in the success of Thomas Seymour's machinations to overthrow his brother, Edward Seymour. Usurping supreme power, he would be in control of the eleven-year-old King and could arrange a marriage contract for him with Lady Jane.

Meanwhile Thomas Seymour had been covertly enriching himself by various illicit means – and now had a princely sum at his disposal. He had accomplished this in part by turning a blind eye to the activities of pirates in return for a share of their ill-gotten gains. He had also inherited all the wealth of his late wife Katherine and so now, with the support of a small group of power-hungry nobles, he was poised to strike. Perhaps he had not noticed that his nephew Edward was becoming increasingly wary of him. Gone were the days when the boy had admired his exuberant ways and relied upon his supposed generosity to obtain extra pocket money. Seymour had made repeated attempts to approach Edward when he was alone in order to take the boy into his own custody, but it seemed that Edward always had those about him in a position to protect him. Anticipating the approaching confrontation between the Seymour brothers, various members of the Council warned the Admiral of the utter folly of trying to overthrow the Protector, but to no avail. Nor was Protector Seymour unaware of his brother's devious plots, and he had already made one attempt to send Thomas abroad on business, but again, without success.

The implausible plan which had been simmering in Thomas Seymour's mind for so long involved first of all kidnapping Edward. Once he had the King safely in his possession he would be in an unassailable position to attack his brother, place him in custody or even find a way of accusing him of high treason, and then set himself up as Protector. But when he was unable to find Edward alone, Thomas's fevered brain pitched on a yet more desperate expedient. He would slip into Hampton Court Palace by night, make his way surreptitiously to the boy's bed-chamber, let himself in with a forged key and snatch Edward as he slept. Armed with a pistol in case of trouble and taking two accomplices, he chose 16 January 1549 as the night in which he would execute his plot. All went well until he arrived at the inner door of Edward's bedroom. Whether the boy was fearful or suspicious it is not now possible to know but evidently he had taken the unusual precaution of locking the inner door to his room and placing his small pet dog between the two doors to warn him of impending trouble.

When Thomas Seymour reached the outer door of the royal bedchamber he opened it with his forged key without difficulty. However when he found the inner door was locked – and even worse, a furious animal yapping shrilly and therefore raising the alarm – he panicked. Without a second thought he shot the dog and tried to force the inner door of Edward's bedroom. Within moments Edward's bodyguards were on the scene and Thomas Seymour was caught, pistol in hand and a dead dog at his feet. Despite his lame excuses that he had come to check up on his nephew's welfare, he was arrested.

It is not hard to imagine the shock and shame that Lady Jane felt as news of these things filtered through to her, and she learned that her guardian had been charged with high treason; for any attempted assault on the King's person was regarded as that. Unless some mitigating circumstances were found to excuse such behaviour, he would almost certainly face the death penalty. In order to exonerate themselves Lady Jane's parents, never trustworthy in a crisis, were quick to provide incriminating evidence against the very man whom they had supported; the case against the Admiral looked increasingly solid. Protector Seymour was reluctant to send his own brother to the executioner's block and waited to see if he could spare him. But other members of the Council, particularly John Dudley, Earl of Warwick, the third member of that triumvirate of power effectively ruling the country, placed pressure on him to treat his brother as he would any other traitor. At last Edward Seymour gave in. On 10 March 1549 the young King was asked to give his formal consent to the death warrant for his uncle – a severe sentence. Although he was spared the responsibility of having to sign a warrant, Edward did not demur – perhaps fear, distrust and the memory of a dead pet dog played some part in his decision. Even facing the scaffold Thomas Seymour was unrepentant and was still plotting his brother's overthrow: just before his death he removed two notes from inside his shoe to be given to the King's older sisters, Mary and Elizabeth. These contained instructions on how to continue a rebellion against the Protector.

Following Thomas Seymour's execution the fearless Hugh Latimer preached before the King. One of the few adroit observers of the restless place-seeking that was forever active in the very heart of government, he made penetrating comments on these events. Referring to the Admiral, he described him as: 'a man furthest from the fear of God than any in England – a covetous man – I would wish there were no more in England. He was a seditious man, a contemner of public prayer – I would there were no more in England. Well! he is gone! I would he had left none behind him.'

Sadly, he had indeed left some behind him, as Lady Jane Grey would discover to her cost. Little now remained for her other than to return once more to Bradgate Manor. Jane's reaction to all these traumatic events can only be a matter of conjecture, but they must have afforded her much distress. We can well imagine she would have felt a measure of relief to be back in the peaceful woods of Bradgate, far from such scenes of political intrigue and bloodshed – if only for a temporary period.

The peace of the woods of Bradgate with their autumn shades of reds and golds, the bronze of the bracken clothing the surrounding hills, the deer bounding freely among the rocky outcrops, must have afforded a measure of relief to Jane after her solitary role at the death and funeral of her closest friend, Katherine Parr.

CHAPTER SEVEN

POLITICAL AND RELIGIOUS UPHEAVAL: 1549-1552

To understand the circumstances that shaped the next few years of Lady Jane Grey's life, we must turn aside and look briefly at the political intrigues and the religious developments that were transpiring in the wider sphere of national life during this period. These, together with a medley of attitudes and reactions in the country as a whole, would impact seriously on the girl's future, and therefore form an essential framework for any correct appreciation of Jane's part in the unpredictable drama of the times.

When the Lord Admiral, Thomas Seymour, was executed in March 1549 Edward had been on the throne for just over two years. He was now eleven years of age: a strong-minded boy, he was seriously concerned about the progress of the Reformation of the church – that work of God that had been progressing steadily and quietly not just in political circles, or even in the universities alone, but in many a pulpit, homestead and heart in the land. Edward wished to see the abolition of Catholic practices such as the Mass and the establishment of evangelical traditions in their place.

Soon after this, as a twelve-year-old, Edward wrote a treatise in which he verbally assailed the notion of papal supremacy. His French tutor, Jean Belmain, tried to tone down the indignation with which Edward expressed himself at times, but this treatise, entitled *The Primacy of the Pope*,[1] gives clear evidence of the youth's personal commitment to the evangelical faith. He was fully supportive of those sweeping changes in the religious life of the country championed by his uncle, the Protector, and effected by Archbishop Thomas Cranmer and other Reformers who had come to England at the invitation of the Archbishop – changes that would outflank the entrenched notions of generations.

The earliest change had come in 1547, the year of Edward's accession to the throne. Shocked by the ignorance of much of the clergy – perhaps only one in ten of whom ever preached a sermon – the Archbishop had introduced his *Book of Homilies*. This provided sermon material which was to be read aloud at gatherings for public worship. Legislation to bind the clergy into compliance was also passed by Parliament. The Dissolution of the Chantries also took place in that year. These Chantries were primarily endowments for the purpose of repeating Masses for the souls of the dead. Sometimes, however, the endowment included the added provision of a small religious house or chapel in which such Masses were to be said. Henry VIII had already paved the way for such a dissolution by a Chantries Act in 1545; but then it was for financial and secular reasons. Now the eradication of superstitious errors became an added objective for taking over and dissolving all such endowments even though some had properties which were being used for charitable or educational purposes.

Many who endowed these Chantries did so either to enhance their own profile, or that of their dead relatives, after their death. These people were understandably angered by such measures and the heavy-handed way in which they were imposed, but the Crown, impoverished by foreign wars and particularly the wars against Scotland, was grateful for the income generated by the sale of any land. So too were the gentry whose political support was often purchased by the hand-outs resulting from the sale of any such properties.

In December 1548 a number of prominent bishops, champions of the 'Old Religion', were stripped of their benefices. Stephen Gardiner, who had tried to orchestrate the death of Katherine Parr in 1546, was sent to the Tower, and Bishop Edmund Bonner to the Marshalsea prison. Clergy were now permitted to marry by a further Act of Parliament; and two months later, on 21 February 1549, a law was passed banning all images from places of worship. Church treasures such as ornate candlesticks, relics regarded as holy, beads and crucifixes were dismantled, burnt or hidden away. Obligatory Confession was also to be abolished.

The most radical of all the reforms was the removal of Latin service books, replaced by Cranmer's *Book of Common Prayer*. Use of the Prayer Book, first set before a somewhat bemused and divided Parliament in 1548, was made semi-mandatory by an Act of Uniformity passed in January 1549. The Act was set to come into full force in June of that year.

This first *Book of Common Prayer*, perhaps designed to prepare the way for Cranmer's second and more unashamedly Protestant Prayer Book three years later, was a half-way house in its dealing with the celebration of the Mass, and equivocal in much of its wording. As Cranmer explained to Martin Bucer, the Strasbourg Reformer currently resident in Cambridge, his Prayer Book contained 'concessions which are only to be retained for a time, lest the people, not having yet learned Christ, should be deterred by too extensive renovations from embracing his religion'. At the same time Cranmer had been working on a much-needed revision of canon law, although this was not published at the time.

Such far-reaching alterations in the religious life of the country could not have gained the degree of acceptance that they did in many parts of the land had it not been for a work of God that had taken place one hundred and fifty years previously. The testimony and labours of John Wycliffe and his Lollard[2] preachers during the last decades of the fourteenth century, which had strengthened rather than diminished during the fifteenth, should not be underestimated or overlooked. The same core issues which burned in the hearts of the sixteenth-century Reformers had also motivated the Lollards. They maintained that preaching, rather than the sacraments, should be of paramount importance; the Bible should be freely available to the people in their own tongue; clergy should be able to marry; the Mass with its doctrine of transubstantiation was to be denounced; prayers for the dead, veneration of images, and the confessional were all to be regarded as erroneous.

Understandably the pre-Reformation church did its utmost to suppress the Lollard influence, and the catalogue of martyrs who endured a fiery death rather than abjure their faith makes galling reading. Martyrdoms and persecution became yet more widespread among groups of Lollards in the years immediately prior to the Reformation. In 1517, the very year that Martin Luther nailed his Ninety-five Theses to the door of the Wittenberg church, a certain John Bent of Chirton, near Devizes, was burnt for denying the Catholic doctrine of the Mass. Three years later in April 1520 seven men and women were burnt in Coventry for teaching their children the Lord's Prayer and the Ten Commandments.

Therefore, the Lollard movement may well account for the swift spread of the Reformation truths in England, for these groups of men and women were the most eager to purchase the copies of Tyndale's New Testament smuggled into the country after 1526. On the other hand, the widespread changes that marked the opening years of Edward's reign with the abandonment of the religious structures that had held sway for many generations were by no means universally accepted.

In fact Protector Seymour and his government were heaping up resentment against themselves from among many ordinary men and women who could not accept the pace of change. Unaffected by the message of the Reformation, these people felt that those landmarks of religious rituals in which they had been nurtured, and in which they had long vested their spiritual confidence, were being swept away. They were uneasy and bewildered because the 'Old Religion' had at least provided them with a sense of security and social cohesion. They might not understand the Latin Mass but its mystic overtones had helped to allay, though not to heal, troubled consciences.[3]

Economically also the days were hard. During the first two years of Seymour's Protectorate inflation had doubled the price of even the most basic commodities. The country was impoverished largely because of the Protector's often ruthless obsession with the subjugation of Scotland, in order to gain the coveted marriage contract between the young Mary Stuart and Edward VI. This 'rough wooing', as it became known, had proved as costly as it was ineffectual.

In addition to the religious and economic questions, the peasant population was becoming increasingly restive and angry over other issues, most notably the Enclosures. Wealthy landowners and farmers had been annexing the common land on which the poor relied to pasture their cattle, enclosing it with fences and using it for their own crops, sheep, cattle or deer parks. Whole villages were depopulated in this way as vast areas were commandeered by the rich to provide sufficient grazing for the sheep needed to supply the country's booming wool industry. Angry, homeless and starving, the peasantry organized widespread protests. Trouble over such Enclosures of land threatened to break out in areas as far apart as Cornwall and other western counties and Suffolk and Kent in the east. Seymour, who had shown genuine understanding of the problems of the peasant classes, did not have the backing of his fellow Council members on this matter, for they themselves had been enriched at the expense of the poor. So when the Protector issued urgent proclamations promising redress for all grievances suffered as a result of the Enclosures, his popularity on the Council plummeted.

Documents known as the 'nine letters' have recently come to light. These were, in fact, letters of pardon in the name of the King or in Seymour's own name to the so-called 'rebels', assuring them of Edward VI's merciful attitudes towards them and of his understanding of their plight. But even as the Protector did his best to appease the angry peasant population, he discovered that this increased the instability of his own position. 'Every man of the Council have misliked your proceedings and wished it otherwise,' wrote William Paget, a fellow politician.

Trouble for the Protector was now gathering on every side. Had he possessed the authority over the people that Henry VIII had enjoyed, there would have been little further unrest, but his attempt to placate the peasant classes had left him friendless at a time when he was most vulnerable. And this was not his only problem. The way he had taken charge of the country, virtually acting in a regal capacity, had bred deep resentments among the other members of the ruling Council. Henry VIII had made provision for a regency of sixteen men to govern during Edward's minority but, as we have seen, Seymour had overruled the dead King's wishes. While the Council members were in general agreement with Seymour's policies he had few difficulties, but when he acted against their perceived interests, he was inviting disaster.

Edward Seymour's rival, John Dudley, Earl of Warwick, had been waiting in the wings for his opportunity to seize power, ever expecting that before long events would lead to the Seymour brothers effectually destroying one another. And he was right. The flamboyant Admiral, Thomas Seymour, had amassed a certain popular following in the country, and for a man to send his own brother to an appointment with the executioner (despite it being at Dudley's insistence) shocked even a community in which capital punishment was commonplace. The Protector's popularity in the Council, and to a certain extent in the country as well, had sunk to an all-time low.

But it was Archbishop Cranmer's *Book of Common Prayer* that acted as the catalyst to bring the situation to crisis point. As the June 1549 deadline for the use of the new liturgy approached, angry churchgoers demanded that again the Mass be recited in Latin. In the eyes of the people an English translation of the words seemed to them to rob the rite of its mystical element. Believing that the elements turned into the actual body and blood of the Lord in the celebration of the Mass, they felt the abandonment of the sacrificial aspects of the wording was cheating them out of spiritual benefits.

With both religious and social problems on his hands, Edward Seymour scarcely knew where to turn. The two issues began to merge, although in fact the problem of the Enclosures was quite distinct from the religious unrest erupting in the West Country. Uprisings, fast approaching a state of civil war, soon broke out and mercenary troops were employed to quell the revolts. In Norfolk, under the leadership of Robert Ket, 16,000 men gathered in arms on Mousehold Heath. John Dudley led a contingent to Norfolk and before long the rebellion was crushed with much

bloodshed, and its leaders executed. Young King Edward chronicled all these events in a succinct, though unemotional style.
From infancy he had been schooled to believe that his authority
was second only to God's – to rebel against any of his wishes, in
particular with respect to the new Prayer Book, was a serious
sin in his view:

> 'We swear to you by the living God by whom we reign, ye
> shall feel the power of that same God in our sword, which
> how mighty it is, no subject knoweth; how puissant it is,
> no man can judge, how mortal it is, no English heart dare
> think. Repent yourselves and take our mercy without
> delay.'

The boy would have been well versed in William Tyndale's classic,
The Obedience of the Christian Man, and in particular Tyndale's
definition of kingship, 'God hath ... in all lands put kings, gov-
ernors and rulers in his stead... Whosoever resisteth them,
resisteth God.'

It seems from accounts of the times that the Protector himself
was not conscious of the extent to which public support was
slipping away from him, nor was he sufficiently aware that there
was one in high places constantly plotting his downfall – waiting
only for the strategic moment to strike. Not only did John Dudley,
Earl of Warwick, take advantage of Edward Seymour's current
unpopularity, he had secretly been undermining him in the
affections of his nephew, Edward VI. Protector Seymour had
persisted in treating the King as a child – which indeed he was –
but he had handled him unwisely, allowing him little share in
government and making proclamations in his name without even
consulting him. Precocious and highly aware politically, Edward
resented this. As we have seen, it was at this very point that his
other uncle, Thomas Seymour, had tried to worm his way into
Edward's favour. John Dudley, however, used another method
of gaining Edward's good will: he made a show of taking the
boy's views and thoughts into serious consideration, treating
him with deference and consulting him over difficult decisions.

Not until early October 1549 did Seymour realize the degree of his unpopularity. In panic he tried to do the very thing that his brother had done a few months earlier – to snatch Edward and keep him in his immediate control, making out that he was defending him against some insurrection. Before attempting to seize the boy his first move was to establish armed support around Hampton Court Palace, where Edward was living. This accomplished, he sent messengers to the Council members informing them that he had the King in his possession and demanding their loyalty and allegiance. But one by one even his supporters slipped away and joined the 'opposition' led by John Dudley.

After waiting for several days without any reply, the Protector realized at last that he was in real danger and so in desperation roused Edward from his bed one night. Persuading the boy that a rebellion was afoot which planned to take his life, he allowed Edward to arm himself with a sword, placed him on horseback and, together with a few household staff, they pushed their way through the crowd that had gathered around Hampton Court. As he passed through Edward made a short impromptu speech, calling out in conclusion, 'Will ye help me against those who would kill me?'

Assured of the loyalty of his subjects, the King and his party rode sixteen miles through the cold October night to Windsor Castle – then surrounded by forest. Edward, who was not yet twelve years of age, was clearly frightened by the experience – one that reminded him vividly of that previous night-time assault by his other uncle only ten months earlier. Before long, Seymour summoned Archbishop Thomas Cranmer and other supporters to join him at Windsor.

After two or three days of negotiations between the Privy Council and those still supporting the Protector at Windsor, a compromise solution was hammered out. If Seymour would submit to the formality of a 'mock' arrest, he would not be punished for his treatment of the King. With his safety apparently assured, Seymour agreed to meet his fellow Councillors to discuss their grievances. But it was a trick for shortly afterwards he found himself conducted to the Tower of London, with a list of twelve offences drawn up against him. His life hung in the balance and it was only the intervention of the young King, horrified at the turn of events, that saved Seymour from following his brother to the block. A 'coup' had been effectively staged. Seymour remained in the Tower and John Dudley, Earl of Warwick, known as the iron man of Tudor politics, took over the functions of the Protector.

Only when John Dudley had secured his own authority, both on the Council and in the country, did he agree to release former Protector Seymour in the spring of 1550, allowing him to resume his seat on the Council. Seymour may well have thought he was now safe but once more it was a ruse: in fact Dudley was playing for time so that he could destroy his main rival. When Dudley married his eldest son to Seymour's daughter Anne, a wedding which was attended by the King, it might have seemed to Seymour that a reconciliation between the two men was complete. It was not. Throughout 1550 Seymour gave Dudley little opportunity to pin any accusations of treachery upon him. By this time Dudley had added to his political stature by claiming one of the four dukedoms in the whole country – the first man ever to hold a dukedom who could not boast royal lineage. Instead of being Earl of Warwick he now became Duke of Northumberland.

Described by a modern writer as 'greedy and rapacious, corrupt, cruel and unscrupulous',[4] and by an earlier historian as 'a man of no principle at all except selfish ambition',[5] Dudley, now in his late forties, was a restless schemer. Dark, handsome, and athletic in his younger days, he had risen swiftly to power under Henry VIII. Although John Dudley shamelessly ousted Seymour from his position, and has generally been perceived as an unprincipled power-seeker, posterity has probably not done justice to the true characters of these two players in the power game of Edward's reign. Some of Seymour's social policies had been ill-advised, and his Scottish wars had brought the economy into dire straits. Quieter and more subtle than either of the Seymour brothers, John Dudley aimed – though with little success – to restore the prosperity of the country by withdrawing from some of the foreign policies that were draining the exchequer of its reserves. However, self-interest was paramount in Dudley's schemes, and the political advancement of his own five good-looking sons was a strong second on his agenda.

In contrast to Seymour's method of governing the country, Dudley now adroitly maintained that there was no such position as 'Lord Protector'. Members of the Council would share power equally, or so he said, while Edward VI was to be brought into greater prominence, attending Council Meetings and ratifying decisions. Dudley knew that he must always act behind the scenes, using the young King as his spokesman. His interviews with Edward were skilfully managed, for he took care not to be seen in consultation with him. Instead he arrived in Edward's bedchamber late at night, when there was no one around to gossip about his activities. Dudley would then brief the boy on the events of the day in the Privy Council and advise him how best to respond to various matters about which he was required to comment.

Effectively Dudley was ruling the country himself, largely making Edward merely his mouthpiece. By gaining the King's absolute confidence and trust and keeping him informed on all matters of state, he avoided the mistakes that Protector Seymour had made. Not only did Dudley know how best to appeal to Edward's self-esteem, he also gave time and attention to pleasing the youth by arranging enjoyable sporting events for him. More than this, he pressed ahead even faster than Seymour had done with the programme of church reform – a concern that lay nearest to Edward's heart. Professing to be an evangelical, Dudley's unswerving support for Reformation principles could only commend him in Edward's eyes.

Edward VI, for his part, was fast becoming a young adult, taking increasing interest in affairs of government and making many plans for the future ordering of his country. He intended to put these into place when he took over the reins of power. With the agreement of the Council this was scheduled to take place on his sixteenth birthday in October 1553. It is not surprising, therefore, that the King rested complete confidence in Dudley, although it was noted by those who observed Edward that he never seemed to be truly relaxed in Dudley's presence – overawed by his dominant personality.

Meanwhile, after his release early in 1550, the former Protector had been careful to avoid any circumstances that might give Dudley a pretext for ousting him yet further from power. But during 1551 Seymour began to lay secret plans in an attempt to regain his lost prestige. The progress of his endeavours was suddenly cut short, however, by a wandering and probably neurotic woman. In September of that year she reported that she had heard a strange 'voice'. This voice warned her: 'He whom the King did best trust will deceive him and work treason against him.' Her strange prophecy was brought to the attention of the new Duke of Northumberland, John Dudley. To whom could it refer? He chose to interpret the uncanny message as a reference to Seymour; mainly because it gave him an excuse for destroying his rival as soon as he could.

In 1549 Seymour had faced unrelieved hostility from the other members of the Privy Council over the Enclosures because he had supported the cause of the common people. Now, in 1551, as he schemed ways of returning to power, Seymour looked to the people for their support in return – a democratic statesman before his day. But as rumours of his manoeuvres began to leak out, it became obvious, at least from the point of view of Dudley and the other members of the Council, that Seymour had become a dangerous man and an unpredictable politician. In the rough justice of the times, he was a man who must be eliminated.

Therefore, in October 1551, Dudley put into action the plot he had been hatching to rid both himself and the country of Edward Seymour. On the night of 13 October he poured into King Edward's ear a tale of intermingled truth and error, coupled with conspiracy and evil intent. Edward wrote down all he had been told in his journal. According to Dudley, the former Protector had been laying careful plans to raise a rebellion, encouraging the people among whom he was still popular to rise in his favour in order to re-establish his control of the country. This much was in fact true but whether he then intended to seize the Tower of London, using the massed weaponry stored there to arm his forces, as Dudley alleged, is less certain. The rest of Dudley's tale most certainly sounds like fabrication. Next, so he told the King, his uncle planned to gather together all members of the ruling Council who had opposed him when he was Protector and have them assassinated, possibly by arranging to have them all poisoned. He then intended to break up Edward's recently contracted marriage to a French princess and marry him to his own daughter. Such allegations bordered on the preposterous and Edward could not and would not believe that his uncle had been guilty of such duplicity, despite the fact that he had little personal affection for him.

In the summer of that year – 1551 – there had been an outbreak of the 'sweating sickness'. No respecter of estate or wealth, this disease – the fourth epidemic of its kind to break out that century – had taken a heavy toll on human life. The victims of 'sweating sickness' would experience, in quick sequence, violent headaches, dizziness and collapse. Then came the drenching sweat that gave the disease its name. Sufferers usually died within twenty-four hours – but if they survived longer, a complete recovery was the norm. The young King had been hastily evacuated to Hampton Court with a minimum staff, while his courtiers and politicians also fled the city.

The 'sweating sickness' was still rife in September 1551, and members of the former Protector's household had been ill with the disease. Postponing his attendance at the Council session due to begin on 13 October, Seymour waited, so he said, until all danger of infection had passed before leaving his country home. But the Council did not accept this explanation for his non-appearance, and when the unfortunate man arrived three days later, apologizing for his absence, he was summarily arrested, accused of treason, and escorted to the Tower once more – soon to be joined by his wife and family.

Seymour's trial was conducted in secret rather than before both Houses of Parliament, as was the normal protocol for such high-profile cases. Papers relating to it were subsequently destroyed; witnesses were unable to agree on the evidence, and Seymour himself repeatedly affirmed his allegiance to the King. For his part, Edward was unwilling to sign or grant any death warrants for his uncle or for his uncle's supposed conspirators. For the first time in his life he asserted his own authority over that of John Dudley – who promptly fell into an uncontrolled rage. Eventually Seymour was found 'guilty' on a number of counts of 'felony' – a term that seemed to embrace a wide variety of possible offences. The end was predictable. Edward pleaded for his uncle's life, and Dudley assured the boy that he was trying his best to save him, but at the same time was feeding Edward with frightening stories of his uncle's treachery.

The King became very depressed and troubled, but made several attempts to avert the impending disaster. It is thought that in the end he may well have been tricked into agreeing to Seymour's execution on the pretext that by it he was serving God and preserving his kingdom from evil. On 22 January 1552 Edward Seymour – the 'Good Duke' as he was dubbed – was executed amid scenes of mayhem and confusion as the people made a desperate attempt to rescue him from the scaffold. 'His blood will make my Lord of Northumberland's pillow uneasy,' said one nobleman with more insight than others. And so Seymour died, protesting to the last his faith in God and his loyalty to his nephew.

CHAPTER EIGHT
'THAT NOBLE AND WORTHY LADY'

Throughout the period from 1549 until early 1553, Lady Jane Grey was living in partial obscurity in Leicestershire; far from the intrigues of court life and quietly continuing her education with her tutor John Aylmer. As an eleven-year-old she had returned to Bradgate Park shortly after the execution of Thomas Seymour and, apart from her social visits to London together with her parents and sisters, would only learn at second hand of the unfolding scenario of events that were shaking the country.

With Edward Seymour's fall from power, Jane's prospective marriage contract with his son, whom she had known for a number of years, was being played down by her parents, Henry and Frances Grey: it no longer being an attractive proposition to them. In common with the practice of the period Jane's own feelings or preferences were not considered in the matter; particularly as she was still only a child. But the truth remains that their highly intelligent and serious-minded daughter had little place at all in Henry and Frances Grey's affections. To them the girl was a failure and any chance of making an advantageous marriage seemed more remote than ever. Jane appeared friendless. Both her guardian Thomas Seymour, and her closest friend Katherine Parr, were dead; there was no voice to plead Jane's case either in court or at home.

Nothing Jane could do seemed to win her any favours in her parents' eyes. Both her father and mother found their pre-eminent enjoyment in field sports; spending many days fishing, hawking or hunting deer in the parkland surrounding Bradgate Manor. When they were not so engaged much of their time was spent at the gambling table, playing for lucrative stakes. Jane, quiet, studious and thoughtful, had neither the aptitude nor inclination for her parents' interests. She soon discovered that everything she did seemed to annoy them: whether she ate or drank, was cheerful or sad, danced or sewed; as she herself later complained, the result was always the same. She would find herself vilified, threatened, mocked and even beaten.

Such circumstances sent Jane ever more frequently to that strong source of consolation for the Christian, the presence and sustaining power of Christ. Since her days in the service and company of Katherine Parr, Jane's faith was becoming ever more earnest and vibrant. Unlike her parents, who had only a nominal adherence to Protestant thought, Jane's views were clear and defined. The truths of the gospel were all-important to her; she read the Scriptures diligently, using her Greek to help her understand the New Testament. Through the harsh experiences of her life, she was learning the way into God's presence in prayer, seeking him for the strength she needed. Words such as these, taken from a later recorded prayer, could well have first arisen from such experiences in childhood:

'O merciful God, consider my misery, best known unto thee; and be thou now unto me a strong tower of defence, I humbly require thee. Suffer me not to be tempted above my power, but either be thou a deliverer unto me out of this great misery, or else give me grace to bear thy heavy hand and sharp correction...'[1]

Dr Thomas Fuller, seventeenth-century preacher and historian, wrote of Jane's parents: 'They were in no whit indulgent to her in childhood but extremely severe, more than needed to so sweet a temper... As the sharpest winters cause the more fruitful summers, so the harshness of her breeding compacted her soul to the greater patience and piety.'[2]

But the picture is not entirely black; her two personal attendants, Mistress Ellen and Elizabeth Tylney, loved Jane dearly, and she loved them in return. Surprisingly, there was another who had an affection for Jane: none other than the Lady Mary,

Edward and Elizabeth's half-sister. Mary's life had been hard: dogged by ill-health and badly treated by her father, Henry VIII, she presented a somewhat pathetic figure. She drew her chief comfort from a twisted and extreme Catholicism, a passionate loyalty to all things Spanish and to the religion of her rejected mother, Katherine of Aragon. When she was in residence Mass might be repeated as often as six times a day in her chapels, and this in spite of the ban imposed on the rite by the Act of Uniformity of 1549.

Now a lonely and bitter woman of thirty-four, Mary still had a tender spot for her young half-brother, King Edward. Assuming that the religious changes introduced during her brother's minority were the work of men such as Thomas Cranmer, John Knox (recently arrived in London at the invitation of the Duke of Northumberland) and other Reformers, she would have hoped that when Edward came of age he would revoke such measures. The prohibition against the celebration of Mass was one that distressed her deeply.

Almost old enough to be Jane's mother, Mary had also shown affection for the child. They had met on many occasions, particularly before the death of Henry VIII when Jane had lived at court with Katherine Parr. Jane's mother, Lady Frances Grey, and Mary were first cousins and much the same age. We know that on one occasion Frances took her three daughters, Jane, Katherine and Mary, to stay with the princess for a few weeks at her London home in Clerkenwell. With her customary generosity, Mary had given Jane a dainty necklace made of pearls and rubies.

Much of Jane's life was uneventful during 1550. Now and then she would spend time at Dorset House, her family's London home, sometimes attending state occasions at court. She now saw less of Edward for as he grew up the responsibilities of kingship were preoccupying him. Jane's happiest hours were spent studying with her tutor John Aylmer. His kindly approach to his gifted pupil presented a sharp contrast to the rebukes and criticisms which she regularly received from her parents.

One day, however, during the late summer of 1550, when all the family apart from Jane were out hunting in the park, an unexpected visitor cantered up the long driveway to Bradgate Manor, riding between the long rows of trees. Roger Ascham[3] had recently relinquished his position as the Lady Elizabeth's personal tutor in Greek and Latin, for the princess was now seventeen and her education was almost complete. A warm friend of the Reformation, Ascham was about to leave the country for a post as secretary to the English ambassador in the court of the Emperor Charles V in Hapsburg. Although he was initially famed for the first work in English on the subject of archery, Ascham was equally interested in the theory of education – an interest he shared with Jane's tutor, John Aylmer. Some years earlier Jane's father, Henry Grey, had also employed Ascham to teach his daughters the skills of writing. And now he had come to say goodbye to the family and to his friend John Aylmer.

Reining in his horse and walking all around the deserted Manor House, Ascham was surprised and disappointed to find no one at home. At last he saw someone in the servants' quarters and asked if she knew where the family had gone. All were out hunting, the girl told him – all, that is, except for one – he would find twelve-year-old Lady Jane studying in her tower room. Making his way up the winding stairs to the tower chamber, Ascham discovered the girl, and to his amazement found her absorbed in reading Plato's *Phædo* in Greek 'with as much delight as some gentlemen would read a merry tale in Boccaccio',[4] as he later reported.

'What are you doing here?' he asked in surprise. 'Why are you not out in the park enjoying yourself with the others?'

'I wist [know] all their sport in the park is but a shadow to that true pleasure I find in Plato,' replied Jane seriously. 'Alas, good folk, they never felt what true pleasure meant.'

Astonished at such a reply from so young a girl, Ascham began to question Jane more carefully.

'And how came you, Madam, to this deep knowledge of pleasure, and what did allure you into it, seeing not many women, [and] but very few men, have attained thereto?'

All the pent-up sorrows of Jane's short life were compressed into her reply; here was someone who might understand her. Her answer has become a classic statement on her life and character, remembered and quoted many years later by Ascham in his most famous book on the theory of education which was published posthumously and called, as part of a longer title, *The Scholemaster*:[5]

> 'I will tell you, and tell you the truth, which perchance ye will marvel at. One of the greatest benefits that ever God gave me is that he sent me so sharp and severe parents and so gentle a schoolmaster. For when I am in the presence of either Father or Mother, whether I speak, keep silence, sit, stand or go, eat, drink, be merry or sad, be sewing, playing, dancing, or doing anything else, I must do it as it were in such weight, measure, number, even so perfectly as God made the world; or else I am sharply taunted, so cruelly threatened, yea, presently sometimes with pinches, nips and bobs [blows] and other ways (which I will not name for the honour I bear them), so without measure misordered, that I think myself in hell, till time come that I must go to Mr Aylmer, who teacheth me so gently, so pleasantly, with such fair allurements to learning, that I think all the time nothing that I am with him. And when I am called from him, I fall on weeping because whatever I do else but learning is full of grief, trouble, fear and wholly misliking to me.'[6]

Referring back to Plato's *Phædo*, Jane concluded,

> 'This my book hath been so much my pleasure and bringeth daily to me more pleasure, and more than that, in respect of it all other pleasures in very deed be but trifles and troubles unto me.'

This outburst, a snapshot into Jane's unhappy home life, natu-rally tells only one side of the story. There is no evidence to suggest that the Marquess and his wife treated their other two daughters in the same way as Jane. To their credit they gave their small hump-backed child Mary the same educational opportunities as they had given the other two – an unusual step in a day when physical deformities were regarded with distaste. Katherine seems to have been a favourite, and a girl who shared her parents' interests in a way that Jane did not. As we have seen, Henry and Frances Grey, whose overweening ambition and pride drove them even to the point of selling Jane's marriage rights for £2000, had faced bitter disappointment over her. Added to this, Jane's earnest Christian faith brought about those family divisions of which Christ himself spoke when he warned that a day would come when faithfulness to the truth would set even 'a daughter against her mother' and 'a man's foes will be those of his own household'.

At the time of this recorded interview with Roger Ascham there had been a further cause of dissension in the family. The current resident chaplain, James Haddon,[7] was strongly op-posed to Henry and Frances Grey's addiction to the gambling table, and with an unusual degree of courage had openly rebuked his patrons from their own pulpit. To placate him, Henry Grey had forbidden any of the domestic staff to join in the pursuit, but he and his wife were quite unwilling to relinquish their pleas-ures and both continued in their gambling. John Aylmer, the tutor, and Jane herself, had both supported Haddon's position, naturally increasing the family rift.

Another factor in the equation of Jane's troubles with her parents must be found in Jane herself. Those who have retold her story in the past have tended to set her up as a model of meekness and godliness. It must be remembered, however, that she was still only a child at this time and a Tudor child as well – with all the characteristics of that distinguished family: highly articulate, strong-minded and determined – even stubborn. It is likely that she was not as compliant with her parents' wishes as she might have been, and as she grew older may well have expressed her views with unusual, even annoying, lucidity. Her convictions were strong and noble, but there was also a rigidity and single-minded zeal about the way in which she followed a course of action she felt to be right – regardless of the feelings of others. Such reactions may have partially contributed to the breakdown of relationships between Jane and her worldly-minded parents.

Roger Ascham could not put the interview with Jane out of his mind. Referring back to it many years later, he commented, 'I remember this talk gladly, both because it is so worthy of memory and also because it was the last talk that ever I had and the last time that ever I saw that noble and worthy lady.'[8] After leaving England he had begun to write to the girl from Germany; it was the start of one of the most surprising corre-spondences ever recorded, not just between Ascham and Jane but between the twelve-year-old and other Reformers on the Continent. 'Go on thus, O blessed virgin', urged Ascham, 'to the honour of thy country, the delight of thy parents, thy own glory, the praise of thy preceptor, the comfort of thy relatives, and the admiration of all' – a stiff demand for a girl who had by then just turned thirteen. And to Jane's tutor, John Aylmer, Ascham wrote in equally dramatic terms: 'O happy Aylmer! to have such a scholar and to be her tutor. I congratulate both you who teach and she who learns.' He continued by asking Jane to correspond with him in Greek, and suggested she also wrote to Johann Sturm, Rector of the Protestant University in Stras-bourg and a former friend of Martin Luther.[9]

Another leading Reformer with whom Jane frequently corre-sponded during 1550, and until his death in 1551, was Martin Bucer,[10] also of Strasbourg. Exiled from his homeland in 1548, Bucer had responded to an invitation from Thomas Cranmer to come to England as Regius Professor of Divinity at Cambridge. Here, until his death in 1551, he aided Cranmer in the produc-tion of the revised *Book of Common Prayer* (published eventually in 1552). During the last year of his life Bucer had corresponded regularly with Jane Grey. Referring to his concern for her, Jane would later describe Bucer as 'that learned and holy father who night and day to the utmost of his ability supplied me with all necessary instructions and directions, and by his advice promoted and encouraged my progress in piety and learning.'[11] Sadly none of the correspondence between them has survived.

These Reformers were lavish in their praise of this unusual girl, both in their correspondence with each other and even with Jane herself. Flattery has never been of benefit to anyone, and Jane must have found it hard to steel herself against eulogistic comments such as words in a further letter from Ascham, addressed to both Aylmer and herself. 'What a divine maid, diligently reading the divine *Phædo*... In this respect you are to be reckoned happier than [the fact] that by father and mother you derive your stock from kings and queens...' he wrote to Jane. About Aylmer he wrote, 'Madam, how fortunate you are in such a master – all joy to you both.' However, Jane's pleasure derived from reading the *Phædo* is not altogether surprising given her early mastery of Greek and the philosophical turn of mind engendered by the Renaissance and encouraged among educated people. In it Plato discourses at length on the immortality of the soul, and demonstrates that the soul is the deathless inhabitant of the body. Thoughts of death and the hereafter were not strange to a child in Jane's circumstances. Had she not been the sole mourner at the funeral of Katherine Parr? The martyrdom of Anne Askew and later the execution of her guardian, Thomas Seymour, must have affected her profoundly. But more than this, she took the philosopher's arguments and clothed them with scriptural content. The joys of heaven in store for the believer, and the ultimate knowledge of the love of God in Christ, gave this young Christian grace to live by however difficult her circumstances.

In common with the nobility of the day, the Marquess and his wife spent much time in travelling from place to place, throwing lavish receptions for aristocratic guests, entertaining and being entertained. Still determined to keep Jane in the public eye whenever they could, they insisted on their daughter attending all these functions, which often involved long nights of revelling. Never robust physically and also emotionally highly-strung, Jane's health may well have suffered as a result. After one particular round of social junketing in October 1550, she was taken ill – possibly due in part to exhaustion. When the 'sweating sickness' broke out in the July of the following year, 1551, Jane's mother succumbed to the disease. As she lay in extreme weakness, she asked for Jane, then aged thirteen, to come and nurse her. Some historians have seen a malevolent significance in this, but that is probably not the case. Instead it could well be a tacit acknowledgement of the qualities of character that were marking out her eldest daughter.

Frances Grey recovered, and soon after the family began to prepare for an important social occasion. They were due to attend a State banquet to be held in honour of the visit of Mary of Guise, Queen Regent of Scotland, who was passing through London on her way back to Scotland from France. She had spent a year visiting her young daughter, Mary Stuart, who was being brought up in the French royal household. Lady Mary Tudor, elder daughter of Henry VIII, always noted for her fondness for fine clothes, heard that Jane had been invited to attend the function, and one day a large parcel was delivered to Bradgate Manor – addressed to the girl. Perhaps, thought Lady Mary, Jane would be pleased with a new dress for the occasion.

As Jane opened the parcel she gazed in amazement at the delicate fabric: 'tinsel cloth of gold and velvet, laid on with parchment lace of gold'. Unfolding the exquisite garment, she scarcely knew what to do. Carefully taught that serious Christian girls should dress only in the simplest fashion, Jane was faced with a dilemma. Her own tutor, John Aylmer, had complimented her on her refusal to wear any ornate clothes, especially at a period when other society girls prided themselves in their gorgeous attire and went about 'dressed and painted like peacocks' as Hugh Latimer, court preacher, would say as he inveighed against the worldly fashions of the nobility. Even Jane's cousin the Lady Elizabeth, anxious to regain her reputation for sobriety after the debacle with Thomas Seymour several years earlier, would be unlikely to wear anything more than a plain dress for the occasion. Jane turned a puzzled face to Mistress Ellen, her nurse. 'What shall I do with it?' she asked with a mixture of wonder and dismay.

'Marry, wear it, to be sure!' came Mistress Ellen's answer.

'Nay,' replied Jane, 'that were a shame to follow my Lady Mary against God's word, and leave my Lady Elizabeth, which followeth God's word.' At her mother's insistence Jane wore the dress for the occasion, and with her petite figure, auburn hair and fresh freckled complexion must have looked charming.

By July 1551 Lady Jane's correspondence with the Continental Reformers had increased, and included such men as Heinrich Bullinger,[12] who began to write to her shortly after Bucer's death. She missed Martin Bucer's encouragement and advice and now found in Bullinger a timely replacement. Most of this correspondence is also lost, but three letters which she wrote survive as part of the collection of *Zurich Letters*. A Swiss Reformer, Bullinger had become successor to Zwingli in Zurich following Zwingli's untimely death in battle in 1531. The interest that Reformers such as Bucer and Bullinger took both in the progress of the Reformation of the English Church and in Jane herself were closely connected, for it was rumoured, falsely as we have seen, that she was likely to marry her cousin Edward. 'Oh! if that event should take place, how happy would be the union and how beneficial to the church!' exclaimed another Swiss Reformer, John ab Ulmis, in a letter to Bullinger. Had he known that negotiations were well advanced for a political alliance between France and England by the marriage of Edward to a French princess, he would not have been so happy.

Jane's letters to Bullinger were scarcely letters at all, but more like essays, written mainly in Latin, intermingled with Greek phrases. Writing on 12 July 1551, Jane thanked the Reformer for sending her father a copy of his treatise entitled *Christian*

Perfection. She described the contents as 'pure unsophisticated religion' from which she was 'daily plucking the sweetest flowers, even as I would from a beautiful garden'. Repudiating the praise which her Continental correspondents heaped on the thirteen-year-old, Jane exclaims in her first letter to Bullinger, 'Such of my actions as bear the characteristics of virtue, I must ascribe solely to that great Being who is the author of all my natural endowments. To him, O worthy man, may your prayers be continually directed on my behalf.'

Jane's strength of character and quality of spiritual life is borne out by her unusual ability to remain unspoilt despite such adulation. Probably the constant rebuffs she received from her parents acted as a corrective measure. She continues in this first letter to Bullinger: 'Whatever the divine goodness may have bestowed upon me, I ascribe only to himself as the chief and sole author of anything in me that bears any semblance of what is good.'

In a further letter Bullinger carefully answered Jane's request for guidance on the best way to start learning Hebrew, but these Reformers were equally anxious about her spiritual growth as about her intellectual development. In the summer of 1552 her tutor, John Aylmer, who appears to have had limited understanding of young people, was alarmed to discover that she was showing signs of being a normal fourteen-year-old as well as a scholar. From his perspective she was taking too much interest in her appearance and even concerning herself about such things as jewellery and hair styles. 'At that age,' he wrote, 'all are inclined to follow their own ways.' Knowing Jane's respect for Bullinger, he asked the Reformer to give the girl some guidance in these matters and especially on how long she should spend on her music – a pastime that afforded Jane much pleasure. Her love for playing the lute gave her some relief from the perplexities of her life, and we can imagine her satisfaction when Bullinger replied, quoting from Plato himself: 'Musical training is a more potent instrument than any other, because rhythm and harmony find their way into the inner places of the soul.'

Nevertheless, he urged her to stronger measures of faith and zeal.

In reply Jane wrote: 'You exhort me to embrace a genuine and sincere faith in Christ my Saviour. I will endeavour to satisfy you in this respect as far as God will enable me to do; but as I acknowledge faith to be his gift, I ought to promise only so far as he may see fit to bestow it upon me. I shall not however cease to pray ... that he may of his goodness daily increase it in me.'

Jane sent small gifts to her correspondents, clearly designed for their wives: perhaps some attractive gloves she had embroidered, or a handkerchief. Writing to Bullinger in the final letter that has survived, Jane confesses: 'My mind is fluctuating and undecided for while I consider my age, sex and mediocrity, or rather infancy in learning, each of these things deters me from writing... As long as I am permitted to live, I shall not cease to offer you my good wishes...'[13]

Not surprisingly after a correspondence with such men as Martin Bucer and Heinrich Bullinger, Jane would be totally convinced of the scriptural teaching on the sacrament of the Lord's Supper. With the rediscovery of biblical truths at the time of the Reformation, this doctrine held a pre-eminent place in the testimony of the men with whom she corresponded. Many in Henry VIII's reign had already gone to the stake, refusing to accept the Catholic teaching of transubstantiation celebrated in the Mass which asserted that the bread and wine actually became the physical body and blood of the Lord. Strongly repudiated by evangelicals, such teaching was regarded as little short of blasphemous.

In a fierce confrontation with his older sister, Edward had forbidden Mary to celebrate Mass – even in private. The brother and sister, both children of Henry VIII, and each with his inherited strength of will, stood face to face and battled out the issue. Though Edward loved his older sister and wept over having to confront her in this way, he was uncompromising in his position. He knew that Mary would not be content merely to celebrate the Mass in private, but that she had a hidden agenda: she wished to be the figure head of a movement to promote a return of the people of England to the old faith. Indeed, there were many, disturbed by the religious changes that had been introduced, ready to rally to her cause.

Despite Edward's prohibition, Lady Mary continued to hear Mass in her chapels and it is in the light of this fact that a scenario involving Jane takes on more significance. In the summer of 1552 the Grey family went to stay with the Lady Mary at another of her palaces, this time at Newhall Boreham in Essex. Jane happened to be passing by the open door of the chapel in company with Lady Wharton, one of Mary's lady companions. There, displayed on the altar in the chapel, was the Host – the wafer of bread that had been consecrated, and had therefore become, according to Catholic teaching, the actual body of Christ. As Lady Wharton passed the door she dropped a curtsey to the Host. Noticing this, Jane asked innocuously, 'Why do you curtsey? Has my Lady Mary come in?'

'No', replied Anne Wharton, 'I make my curtsey to him that made us all.'

'Why,' asked Jane provocatively, 'how can that be, when the baker made him?'

Jane's remark was regarded as highly offensive and reported immediately to Mary herself, who, we are told, 'never after loved the Lady Jane as she had done before'.[14] Not only does such a remark reveal a quick-thinking mind, it also shows that under Jane's quiet outward demeanour was a young person of fearless disposition who was prepared to stand by her convictions even if it cost her the friendship of one who had shown her kindness.

CHAPTER NINE

EDWARD AND JANE –
IN STRENGTH AND WEAKNESS

If the Reformers heaped adulation on Jane, she was quite able to return the compliments: 'Were I indeed to praise you as truth requires, I should need the eloquence of Demosthenes or Cicero ... but I am too young and ignorant for either,' she told Heinrich Bullinger. 'Besides,' she added, 'I cherish the hope that you will pardon the more than feminine boldness of an untaught girl who presumes to write to a man who is a father in learning.'

As 1552 progressed, Lady Jane, who was now fourteen, moved from childhood to young adulthood – for it seemed there was no place for adolescence among the Tudor nobility, or, indeed, within society as a whole. By that age many girls of her social standing had already been married off, generally to husbands whose prestige would enhance the status of their parents – yet Jane, due to celebrate her fifteenth birthday in October, remained unmarried. As we have seen, she had been contracted to Edward Seymour, oldest son of the former Protector, but the misfortunes of that statesman who had previously ruled the country with little short of regal control, meant that her parents were now in no hurry to arrange for the marriage to go ahead. Honouring such commitments appeared to have little place in the thinking of Henry Grey and his wife.

With John Dudley now holding the title Duke of Northumberland, and in a position of supreme power, the political landscape had changed radically since Jane had left London. The Duke had packed the Privy Council with his supporters, adding twelve new names to the original sixteen established by Henry VIII. Resourceful and clever, he seemed unassailable. His foreign policy appeared successful, although his devaluation of the currency had only produced yet more economic hardship, as prices of essential commodities rose to three times what they had been at the end of Henry VIII's reign. He had, however, made many enemies as he relentlessly pursued the path to total dominance. The Earl of Arundel was not the only one of Protector Seymour's former supporters languishing in prison because he would not support the Duke of Northumberland's bid for pre-eminence. His cruel suppression of the peasants in the uprisings over Enclosures in 1549 was one that would be long remembered against him, making him deeply unpopular in the country as well as among his fellow Council members. Northumberland's rule was one of fear, purchasing support for his policies through the sale of church lands to those whose assistance he needed.

Another who had much cause for animosity towards the Duke of Northumberland was the Lady Mary, Edward's VI's half-sister and next in line to the throne. His treatment of Katherine of Aragon's daughter had been uncharitable and tactless. A strong bond of affection had once existed between the young King and Mary, but the Duke had frustrated Mary's every attempt to contact her younger brother or to visit him at court. She had heard rumours that if she ever attempted to come to London she would be forced to attend a Protestant service – a possibility repugnant enough to Mary to ensure that she kept her distance. Her priests, whose function it was to perform the rite of the Mass for Mary, were hassled and even imprisoned. She herself had made an abortive attempt to flee the country, but even though all arrangements were in place for her escape, she lost her nerve and abandoned the scheme at the last moment. If ever a circumstance arose that Mary should come to the throne, John Dudley, Duke of Northumberland, would know for certain that his days were numbered.

By 1552 Edward was making more decisions on his own behalf. In February of that year, shortly after the execution of Edward Seymour, Bishop Nicholas Ridley had preached a sermon on the duty of the Christian to care for the poor: a need that had become yet more urgent in view of the dissolution of the Chantries. Many of these had once had hospitals and

Bishop Nicholas Ridley
He was a great champion for the poor, elderly and dis-
abled. Through Ridley's stirring preaching Edward VI
began two institutions, St. Thomas' Hospital and Christ's
Hospital School, both of which continue today.
   Nicholas Ridley was martyred for his faith in 1555.

educational establishments attached to them. Edward was touched by the sermon, and asked to see Ridley immediately afterwards. In this private interview he asked the bishop to arrange for the endowment of two benevolent institutions. One was to be a hospital for the care of the poor, particularly the elderly and disabled, housed in the disused convent building of St Thomas in the London borough of Southwark. The other was a school for the education of poor and orphaned children, making use of the Greyfriars Convent at Newgate, and named Christ's Hospital School. Both of these foundations continue to the present day.

Edward played an increasingly active part in the progress of the Reformation. When John Hooper, Bishop of Gloucester, refused to sign the Oath of Supremacy at his official confirmation of office because the wording included a reference to 'the saints' as well as to God, the thirteen-year-old Tudor King struck out the offending words with his own hand, much to Hooper's delight. On the other hand, in a disagreement between Archbishop Cranmer and the Scottish Reformer John Knox regarding the decision to retain the instructions to kneel when partaking of the bread and wine at the Communion Service, Edward endorsed Cranmer's view. This highly displeased Knox, who saw it as a remnant of the veneration of the Host in the Catholic service. Knox denounced the decision and the young King even received a mild rebuke from John Calvin himself. The publication of the Prayer Book was delayed and the matter only resolved by the insertion of a last-minute 'black rubric' – an explanatory note against the text, printed in black instead of the customary red used for other such explanations, for time was at a premium.

Many historians have given the impression that Edward had always been a frail child, whose life expectancy was short at best. His fair colouring, inherited from his mother, and his slim physique may have given the impression of delicacy, but his own *Chronicle* with its details of the many sporting events which he enjoyed to the full, gives no impression of the King as the

secluded and sickly boy so often portrayed. Two hours each
day was given to outdoor sports, contests and hunting.

Undeniably, however, there was a history of early deaths
particularly among the male members of the Tudor family. In
the summer of 1551 Lady Jane had lost her two uncles, half-
brothers of her mother, who were both close in age to Jane and
King Edward. Henry and Thomas Brandon, sons of Jane's
grandfather, Charles, had died within two days of each other
during the 'sweating sickness' epidemic; both were highly intelligent, able and serious young men who had studied with Edward
and Jane at Greenwich Palace. Edward had been particularly
fond of Henry Brandon, the older of the two and several years
his senior. The young men had been students at St John's
College in Cambridge when the illness swept through the insti-
tution, robbing the country of some of its ablest youth. As we
have noted, their mother, Catherine, child-bride of Jane's grandfather, was an earnest Christian woman and had been one of
Katherine Parr's ladies-in-waiting.

Undoubtedly Jane would have felt the loss of her childhood
friends. With the death of the two boys there was no one left to
inherit Henry Brandon's title of Duke of Suffolk, which he had
held since the death of his father, Charles Brandon, six years
earlier. The title was therefore conferred to Jane's father, Henry
Grey, currently Marquess of Dorset, even though his only link
with the Brandon family was by marriage. So in 1551 Henry
and Frances Grey became the Duke and Duchess of Suffolk.

Edward's own health had given little cause for anxiety since
his recovery from malaria at the age of four. But in April 1552
the youth was taken ill with an attack of measles – a potentially
serious condition even today. According to Edward's own record
he 'fell sick of the measles and the smallpox'. It is unlikely, however, that his rash was indeed the disfiguring smallpox for three
weeks later he wrote to his sister Elizabeth to say that he had
had 'good escape out of the perilous disease'. His public
engagements began again soon afterwards – perhaps too soon,
and the King was not given the time necessary to recuperate
from the illness.

While Edward was still far from strong, his well-loved tutor, Sir John Cheke, on whom he had depended for advice and support throughout his short life, fell seriously ill. Edward's personal faith shone out at this time as he gave himself to earnest prayer for his tutor's recovery. He felt he needed him, perhaps as a counterbalance to the oppressive influence of the Duke of Northumberland. As the news of Cheke's condition grew graver each day, Edward commented simply, 'I shall continue to pray for him.' At last the physicians broke the news to the King that it was feared that his tutor could not live much longer. To their astonishment the boy replied, 'No, Cheke will not die this time – for this morning I begged his life in my prayers – and obtained it.' Cheke was soon clearly on the path to recovery, and in a few weeks was active again.

As the summer months came on, Edward began a tour of parts of the country, designed to give his countrymen a chance to see their King. This year it was to be of Sussex, Hampshire, Wiltshire and Dorset. A punishing round of social activities, long days spent riding through the countryside, feasting and entertaining far into the night, proved more than Edward could sustain. By August the tour was cut short for it 'had been observed on all sides how sickly he looked, and general pity was felt for him by the people'. The nearest royal palace was Windsor Castle, and although the place had unpleasant memories for Edward, he was too exhausted to travel further. An Italian doctor, Girolamo Cardano, was summoned. Deeply impressed with the qualities of character he noted in his patient, the doctor saw all too clearly that the symptoms of tuberculosis had begun to undermine the young King's body. Although he admitted privately to having seen 'the appearance on his face denoting early death', he feared to tell the Privy Council this diagnosis, and merely ordered as much rest as possible.

Throughout the autumn Edward's condition deteriorated; the periodic fevers, the loss of weight and the distressing coughing of blood announced all too clearly that the Italian doctor's diagnosis had been correct. By Christmas 1552 it was evident to all close to him that the youth was dying. This fact threw John Dudley, Duke of Northumberland, into a dilemma. All his personal ambitions were centred in Edward's continuing reign. He began to write pleasant letters to Mary instead of the offensive missives of the past. Mary, who had deliberately been kept in ignorance of her brother's condition, must have suspected the motives behind such a change of attitude and insisted on being allowed to visit Edward.

As Mary rode into London, accompanied by a large contingent of horsemen, she was further astonished by the courteous welcome afforded to her by the Duke. Soon she saw why. For three days her brother was too ill to receive her, but when Mary finally gained access to Edward's sickroom, his changed appearance shook her profoundly. Was Northumberland indeed preparing to welcome her as the new Queen in the event of her brother's death, or was it a trap? She did not know.

Although Edward managed a last public appearance in February 1553 when he opened Parliament, his condition distressed all who saw him. Shortly after this he left Whitehall Palace for Greenwich Palace – a favourite location. This large country house on the banks of the Thames where his father, Henry VIII, and both his sisters had been born was a place where Edward had spent some of his happiest days as he had mingled with other young people for his lessons. Accompanying Edward to Greenwich was his tutor, Sir John Cheke, and Henry Sidney, one of his closest friends who had once shared lessons in the royal classrooms and was now in his personal service. Edward, still only fifteen years of age, clung to the hope that in the fresh country air he might recover.

Meanwhile the Duke of Northumberland had much thinking to do. If Edward should die and Mary Tudor come to the throne, he would almost certainly lose his head – sooner rather than later. He realized that even his apparent show of pleasantries could not avert his downfall and that of his family with him. He must by some means prevent the throne passing to Mary, but how that could be accomplished in view of the Act of Succession enshrined in Henry VIII's will, he did not see. Gradually a scheme started to formulate in his mind. He began to think of a young girl of fifteen – Lady Jane Grey.

Jane, as we have seen, was third in line to the throne. Should Edward die without heirs, Mary came first, then Elizabeth, then Jane, followed by her sisters. Certainly it would be to John Dudley's advantage to be closely allied to the Grey family at such a time. His youngest son, sixteen-year-old Guilford Dudley, was fair-haired, tall, slim and good-looking; his mother's favourite, and a petulant, spoilt young man. The plan taking shape in his father's mind was to marry Guilford to Jane Grey. If he could then persuade the dying Edward to change his father's Act of Succession, he could arrange for him to leave his throne to Lady Jane, making her Queen of England. John Dudley would then retain his power, with his son Guilford the *de facto* king. He had a plausible case for his scheme because both Mary and Elizabeth were still theoretically disqualified from inheriting the throne, with the declaration of illegitimacy against them never having been repealed.

In the spring of 1553, when Edward's hold of life was frail at best, Northumberland began to put his plan into action. Approaching the new Duke and Duchess of Suffolk, Jane's parents, he proposed Guilford as a suitable husband for Jane. As we have seen, Jane was officially contracted to marry young Edward Seymour, the marriage only delayed because of the Protector's ignominious fall from power during 1549. Despite this fact Henry and Frances Grey acceded to Northumberland's plan and agreed that Jane should be betrothed to Guilford. They must have known that such a proposal would be highly distasteful to Jane.

The Grey family were currently resident at their London home, Suffolk Place, when Jane received a message that her parents wished to see her. Doubtless she prepared herself for the interview with some trepidation. Perhaps they had at last made arrangements for her marriage to Edward Seymour to go ahead. When the proposition was announced to Jane, that she was to marry Guilford Dudley, not as a mere suggestion but as a definite contract, she was stunned. Arranged marriages were the norm among the aristocracy – Jane knew that. But she was already engaged; how could her parents so lightly renege on their pledges? Besides she despised Guilford. Apart from good looks he had few characteristics that could commend him to someone like Jane. Other girls may have wept, stamped, protested: Jane did none of those things. She did the unthinkable. She refused. Such an act of defiance was astonishing in the sixteenth century. Only a slip of a girl, she stood resolute before a bullying mother, whose figure was increasingly resembling that of her uncle Henry VIII for obesity with each passing year. No, she would not marry Guilford Dudley.

Then came the retribution. First her father began to swear and curse, as Jane continued to point out that such a marriage could not take place because she was already engaged. Next her mother took her recalcitrant daughter in hand, and gave the girl such a beating as only a woman of Frances Grey's physique could bestow. It is not hard to imagine the scene afterwards as Jane's kindly attendants gently bathed her aching body and put the bruised girl to bed. Jane had no alternative but to give in. Once she recognized that she was defeated, she behaved correctly towards her parents and towards Guilford – but always keeping him at a distance. How could it be otherwise? The betrothal between the two young people was announced late in April 1553. Thomas Fuller, seventeenth-century writer of *The Worthies of England,* could only comment dryly, 'Whilst a child, her father's house was to her a house of correction, nor did she write *woman* sooner than she could subscribe *wife.*'[1]

CHAPTER TEN
EDWARD'S 'DEVISE'

'I am glad to die,' whispered Edward weakly to himself, as his condition deteriorated rapidly. Only his tutor Sir John Cheke, and his close friend Sir Henry Sidney[1], whom he could seldom bear out of his presence, heard him speak. To men such as John Cheke, who had nurtured and taught Edward from early childhood, the King's debilitating illness was a great sorrow. Not many weeks earlier Cheke had written to a well-wisher who had sent the patient a gift of some books to cheer him:

> 'Should a longer life be allowed him, I prophecy indeed that, with the Lord's blessing, he will prove such a king as neither to yield to Joshua in the maintenance of true religion, nor to Solomon in the management of the state, nor to David in the encouragement of godliness. It is probable that he will not only contribute very greatly to the preservation of the Church, but also that he will distinguish learned men by every kind of encouragement. He has long given evidence of these things...'[2]

But now in late May 1553, these high hopes looked as if they were about to be dashed for it was evident to all about him that the boy could not live much longer. His pains were intense, yet through it all he expressed an unswerving faith in the mercy of God and the sacrifice of Christ as the grounds of his assurance.

The marriage of Lady Jane Grey to Lord Guilford Dudley had taken place a week earlier, on 25 May, but the King had been too ill to attend. The venue for the celebrations was Durham House in the Strand and two other marriages were celebrated on the same day. A further alliance uniting the Grey family yet more closely with the cause of the Duke of Northumberland had been arranged for Jane's younger sister, thirteen-year-old Katherine. She was married to the son of another of Northumberland's stalwart supporters, Lord Herbert, Earl of Pembroke. And lastly, Northumberland's own daughter, also named Katherine, was married to the Earl of Huntingdon's son. A powerful nobleman, Huntingdon owned extensive lands adjacent to those of Henry Grey. Even though he and Henry Grey were long-term rivals, the Earl's wealth and prestige meant that his support was essential to Dudley for the fulfilment of his plans.

For the auspicious occasion Durham House had been newly decorated and hung with exquisite tapestries. Ill as he was Edward took an interest in the proceedings for he had retained his fondness for his cousins, and particularly for Jane. He ordered his Master of the Wardrobe to supply splendid wedding outfits for both the girls and donated many pieces of jewellery to complete their finery. With her long auburn hair entwined with pearls and dressed in a gown of gold and silver brocade, sparkling with diamonds and pearls sewn to the fabric, Jane arrived by barge at Durham House, together with Katherine.

A grand affair, the marriage ceremony was attended by many of the country's prestigious citizens, and was followed by feasting and jousts. Given her reluctance to marry Lord Guilford Dudley we can imagine that such celebrations brought little pleasure to Jane. Perhaps she did not have much appetite for the spiced bridal cakes and other delicacies served at the wedding supper; at least there is no record that she suffered from the food poisoning that laid the young bridegroom low a few hours later. The chef was forced to confess to having put the wrong ingredients into some of the food in error. That night all three brides were parted from their grooms, returning to their own family homes. At Northumberland's decree the marriages were to remain unconsummated for the present so that they could be more easily dissolved should the need arise. The feelings of the young people concerned were of little consequence in such arrangements.

Jane may not have suffered from food poisoning, but shortly after the marriage ceremony she was taken ill. She begged to stay with her mother at their newly acquired property, Sheen Palace, overlooking the Thames: a mansion formerly belonging to the ill-fated Protector Seymour. Normally she would have been expected to stay at Syon House in Isleworth, a one-time monastery turned into a mansion, where Northumberland and his family were in residence; Jane's wish to stay at Sheen indicates the strength of her distaste for the family into which she had been married. In addition, Jane herself was sure she was being poisoned, not accidentally but deliberately, by order of Northumberland. This is unlikely; in fact, it is more probable that she was suffering from a type of dysentery or even nervous exhaustion after all the distress of recent events. It would also appear that Jane – like the rest of the country – was totally unaware of the serious nature of Edward VI's condition; and, strange as it may seem, there is no record extant suggesting that Jane may have guessed the plan that lay behind her sudden forced marriage to Guilford Dudley.

With Edward growing daily weaker, the Duke of Northumberland knew that it would be imperative to act speedily if there were to be any chance of preventing the King's half-sister, Mary, from becoming Queen of England on the death of her brother. She had already shown herself to be unmoveable in her insistence on Catholic dogma, and would clearly use her power to undo all that had been achieved in reforming the church, reversing everything that Edward had lived to accomplish. But worse than this from Northumberland's perspective, his own head would not remain long upon his shoulders if Mary should become Queen.

The Reformation had been steadily progressing since the early decades of the century when Erasmus had published his Greek New Testament. As the Scriptures became freely available in English after the death of Tyndale, it had advanced yet more significantly. Now with the encouragement and support of Edward, and those Reformers surrounding him, its forward march had seemed unstoppable. But if Mary should come to the throne then its progress would receive a severe setback.

Most who record this last grievous period of Edward's life present a picture of the dying King as a powerless and ineffectual pawn in the hand of an ambitious and domineering man. The blame for the scheme to prevent Mary's accession to the throne, and to avert what both Northumberland and Edward regarded as an impending disaster for the work of reforming the English Church, has been laid squarely at the door of the Duke of Northumberland; and with it the whole disastrous chain of events that followed.

Certainly, the initial suggestion to alter Henry VIII's will in an attempt to secure the Protestant heritage came from Northumberland. Edward had always shown high respect for his father and concern to fulfil his wishes, and would certainly have resisted such a course of action. He would be acutely aware of the illegality of changing a document that had been enshrined in an Act of Parliament. But in his weakened condition and with an increasing awareness of how easily all that he had striven to achieve in his six brief years as King could be lost, Edward was clearly open to such a suggestion.

'It is the part of a religious and good prince to set apart all respects of blood, where God's glory and his subject's weal may be endangered...' the Duke had argued. It was Edward's duty, as a Christian king, to put the spiritual needs of his people above all other considerations. And then Northumberland added a cruel stab, 'That your Majesty should do otherwise were, after this life – which is short [and Edward now realized how very short] to expect revenge at God's dreadful tribunal.' This was a callous attempt to intimidate the sick King.

But if Edward disinherited Mary on the grounds of her Catholicism, 'What about Elizabeth, the next in line?' She had given every indication of a total acceptance of Protestant truth. She would know well, at least by repute, that her own mother, Anne Boleyn, had been a sincere convert to the evangelical faith. Northumberland had anticipated such an objection, and had a ready answer. As both princesses had been disinherited by their father, and declared illegitimate by Archbishop Cranmer – Mary in 1533 and Elizabeth in 1536 – neither could theoretically inherit the throne. Northumberland also had a further line of argument with which to persuade Edward. Elizabeth, and Mary too for that matter, would undoubtedly marry a foreign prince, probably a Catholic as well. Such a king would take advantage of his wife and use his position to take over the country, annexing it to his own State. England would then cease to exist as a separate country. The scenario was alarming indeed. Edward needed no more convincing. The only obvious person to succeed him was Lady Jane Grey, now third in line to the throne, although first in strictly legal terms. An earnest Christian, a strong personality and highly able academically, she was well suited for such a role.

Edward might be ill, and even overawed by Northumberland's domineering character, but he had never shown himself weak-willed, and the fact remains that once he had been convinced that he was doing right in the sight of God, he summoned up all the residue of his strength and determined to see the deed accomplished. During the early days of June, Northumberland himself was suffering one of his frequent bouts of illness and could not attend upon the King. This was the period during which Edward was drawing up what he called 'My devise for the Succession'. We must therefore conclude that Northumberland cannot be held solely responsible for the chain of events that would shortly ensue.

Suffering periods of delirium, interspersed with spasms of distressing coughing, in agony with bedsores and ulcers, and rapidly losing the control of his hands, Edward drafted out the new terms for the succession to the throne. The document is still to be seen, written in an unsteady hand with many words scored out.[3] Omissions to the original wording were added when it was pointed out to him that he had in fact left the throne to *Jane's heirs*, and not to Jane herself, so making no provision for any immediate succession in the event of his death. In his final draft Edward specifically named Jane as his heir rather than any sons she might one day bear.

Time was short and the Duke, recovered once more from his indisposition and back at the King's bedside, was anxious to have the document ratified by law. Edward's doctors told Northumberland that the King had perhaps only three days to live – not long enough for all the processes to be accomplished for the 'Devise' to be legalized by Parliament. So the Duke dismissed those responsible doctors who had cared for Edward ever since his birth, and installed a woman quack doctor who claimed to be able to cure the King. It is thought that this quack employed by Northumberland began to poison Edward's system with arsenic in order to staunch the internal haemorrhaging, and so keep him alive a little longer – understandably, this would have caused some of the intolerable suffering that Edward endured in the last days of his life.

On 11 June the Lord Chief Justice, Sir Edward Montague, and other senior lawyers were summoned and Edward's 'Devise' was read out to them. Terrified at the prospect of so flagrant a violation of the law, Montague demurred, protesting that it was illegal. 'I will hear no objections. I command you to draw the letters patent forthwith,' said Edward with all the strength he could command. Pleading for time to consider the King's wishes, these perplexed lawyers withdrew. After some consideration, they returned saying they could not in conscience obey the King in this matter. They feared for their own personal safety, if Northumberland should later decide to betray them. Many tears were shed as the dying King exclaimed in anger and despair, 'Why have you refused to obey my order? To refuse was treason.'

The lawyers pleaded that the 'Devise' could not be ratified without an Act of Parliament and Sir Edward added, 'I have seventeen children. I am a weak old man and without comfort.' He realized all too well what could happen to him if the people rose in favour of Mary's claim to the throne and the King's 'Devise' were overthrown.

'I will have it done now, and afterwards ratified by Parliament,' insisted Edward with increasing urgency and frustration. Only with the Council members loyal to Northumberland standing menacingly in the background, the sick youth in front of them and the promise of a judicial pardon if anything went wrong, did Sir Edward Montague and his fellow lawyers yield to the King's demand and agree to ratify his 'Devise'.

Archbishop Cranmer, who only a day or two earlier had gained Edward's royal assent for his *Articles of Religion*,[4] was also most disturbed at the unconstitutional turn of events. He wished to speak to his dying godson alone in order to try and dissuade him from changing the Succession in such an arbitrary manner; but permission was refused. Edward too added his querulous rebuke, 'Will you alone be more repugnant to my will than the rest of the Council?' Only Cranmer's deep personal affection for his godson who was also his sovereign at last persuaded him to concur with Edward's proposition, and he signed 'unfeignedly and without dissimulation'.[5] How could he add to Edward's distress in the last hours of his life? Cranmer alone had some justification for his position in supporting the 'Devise', for it was he who had declared both Mary and Elizabeth illegitimate at the behest of Henry VIII. On 17 June he added his signature to the document.

Still there were matters to settle. Northumberland could see his whole plan unravelling if the people rallied to the standard of either Mary or Elizabeth. They must both be apprehended if possible, or at least kept in ignorance of their brother's condition until all arrangements were finalized and Lady Jane placed upon the throne. He could not let Edward die yet, although the boy had been unable to eat anything since 11 June. But when at last, despite the administrations of the quack, it became obvious that death was imminent, Northumberland dismissed the woman and her accomplices with all their phoney remedies, and brought back Edward's own doctors to the sickroom. There was little these dedicated royal physicians could now do for their patient other than to make him as comfortable as possible. In his

Archbishop Thomas Cranmer and Edward VI

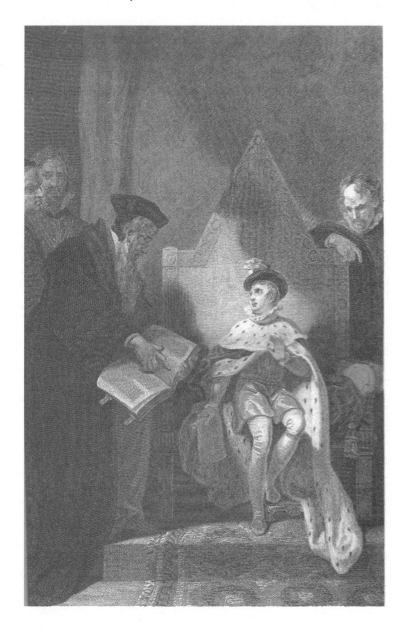

moments of consciousness the fifteen-year-old King could be heard praying quietly:

> 'Lord God, deliver me out of this miserable and wretched life, and take me among thy chosen: howbeit, not my will but thine be done. Lord, I commit my spirit to thee. O Lord, thou knowest how happy it were for me to be with thee: yet for thy chosen's sake, send me life and health, that I may truly serve thee. O my Lord God! bless thy people, and save thine inheritance! O Lord God, save thy chosen people of England! O my Lord God, defend this realm from papistry, and maintain thy true religion; that I and thy people may praise thy holy name, for thy Son, Jesus Christ's sake!'

One of his doctors stood nearby. 'We heard you speak to yourself,' he said, 'but what you said we do not know.' 'I did not know you were so near,' Edward replied simply, 'I was praying to God.'[6]

Sir Henry Sidney, Edward's friend, sat beside him much of the time during the last days of his illness. And on the afternoon of 6 July 1553 Henry gathered up the boy's emaciated frame into his arms. 'I am faint...' murmured Edward. 'Lord, have mercy upon me – take my spirit.' And resting in his friend's arms he gave up his soul to his God. The long struggle was over. A violent thunderstorm broke over London that afternoon, as though symbolic of the stormy years that lay ahead, particularly for men and women who were faithful to the great truths of the Reformation – those truths that had transformed the lives of many in all parts of the land.

CHAPTER ELEVEN
RELUCTANT QUEEN

A lthough rumours had been circulating throughout London and further afield that the King was seriously ill, even dying, few knew the exact position. Until early July Northumberland had been issuing specious bulletins suggesting that Edward's condition was improving for it was imperative to his scheme to keep the true state of affairs concealed for as long as possible. Even Northumberland appeared unready for the speed of Edward's death after the quack doctor left him, although he had received ample warning. A vital part of his strategy to secure the throne had not been accomplished: he had not been able to effect the capture of Mary. So now it was of paramount importance that few, if any, should know that the King had actually died until he was ready to present Lady Jane to the people of London as their new Queen.

Northumberland had another yet more pressing concern: if he allowed Edward's body to be embalmed, as was usual for royalty, it would be immediately evident by its condition that the King had ultimately died of arsenic poisoning. What then could he do with the body of the one who had once been described as England's 'most noble jewel'? Facts are scarce but there is a strong, if somewhat improbable tradition based on a letter later written by one of Northumberland's own sons, that his father ordered Edward should be buried secretly in the paddock behind Greenwich Palace. Another body, that of a murder victim who resembled Edward in some respects, was substituted, quickly laid in a coffin and the coffin sealed, or so the letter stated. However we have neither the means of testing the truth of this tradition nor of knowing whether or not it was Edward's remains that were buried in state several weeks later. Henry Sidney, himself in a compromised position by being married to Northumberland's daughter Mary, left no record of such a substitution taking place; nor did the doctors in attendance, but the days were tumultuous and fear may well have cast a spell of silence over the proceedings.

Northumberland's position was strong – almost inviolable it might have seemed. He controlled the Tower of London which housed a numerous stockpile of weaponry, and in addition the crown jewels and the Royal mint. Windsor Castle was also well stocked with armaments ready in case of need. As word of Edward's death and the change of the Succession in favour of Lady Jane slowly began to leak out, few seriously imagined that Northumberland's plans could be overturned.

Not until two days after Edward had died were his sisters, Mary and Elizabeth, informed and then only when it became clear that the situation could be concealed no longer. Mary immediately began her preparations to come to London in triumph to claim her crown. Meanwhile Northumberland made last-minute arrangements to ensure that all the important members of the Privy Council were sufficiently terrorized by his dominant powers to support his actions; they must oppose Mary and vow loyalty to the little-known Lady Jane, now Lady Jane Dudley, as the next Queen of England. We are told in a contemporary record that they were 'as afraid of Northumberland as mice of a cat'.

Next he must call Jane to come immediately to Syon House where he would inform her that her cousin Edward had bequeathed the crown to her.[1] Jane was currently staying at Chelsea Palace, scene of the much happier days when she had lived with Katherine Parr. She had eventually spent part of the intervening weeks since her marriage at Syon House with her young husband, a circumstance ordered by Northumberland once he was sure the King could not live. But now she was recuperating from another period of illness, and was still convinced that she had been poisoned by her new in-laws. This was an unreasonable assumption for the whole of Northumberland's plan hinged on her well-being, at least for the present.

In the late afternoon of 9 July 1553 Northumberland sent his own daughter Mary, wife of Henry Sidney the dead King's close friend, to Chelsea. She must not tell Jane that Edward had died: that was still a well-guarded secret; nor give any reason for the summons other than she was 'to receive that which had been ordered for me by the King', as Jane afterwards recorded. Jane pleaded her sickness but Mary was insistent; the matter was urgent, she told Jane, and no excuse would suffice. Reluctantly Jane agreed and both girls proceeded by barge up the Thames to Syon House.

Disembarking, they made their way across to the grey, un-inviting building. They entered the impressive entrance hall, now all hung with splendid tapestries, and waited silently. No one seemed to be about: Jane grew ever more apprehensive of the purpose of this strange summons. An intelligent girl, she must have begun to anticipate that there could be some con-nection between the illness of her cousin Edward, her hastily enforced marriage to Guilford Dudley, and this unexpected demand for her presence at Syon. But even should Edward die, Jane knew as well as any citizen in England that Mary was next in line to the throne, and if she had had any prescience of what was awaiting her, she would have banished the thought immediately.

Northumberland finally appeared, accompanied by members of the Privy Council, including Lord Pembroke and the Earl of Huntingdon, both of whose children had recently shared the joint marriage ceremony on the same day as Jane and Guilford. To Jane's astonishment these powerful magnates, symbols of the hierarchy of England, stooped one by one and kissed her small hand. 'With unwonted caresses they did me such reverence as was not at all suitable to my state,' reported Jane later. 'Perhaps it is all designed to mock me,' she thought wildly. Continuing her account, she wrote, 'They were making a semblance of honouring me, calling me their sovereign lady'. Still it appears that Jane did not realize Edward had died. If he had, she reasoned, surely as his cousin, she would have been among the first to know.

As in a daze she heard Northumberland telling her to proceed to the Chamber of State. Entering the august precincts reserved for occasions of high national significance, Jane was further startled to see her own parents, her mother-in-law, the Duchess of Northumberland, and her husband Guilford, all standing waiting to greet her – and beyond, on a dais, an empty throne. No kindly look eased the tension of the occasion, for none of these had ever shown Jane any affection. Bewildered and terrified, her slight form dwarfed by the austere figures of the adults around her, the girl saw John Dudley, Duke of Northumberland, stand forward to address her:

> 'I do now declare the death of his most blessed and gracious Majesty King Edward VI'

were his startling words. He then went on to speak of the exceptional qualities of the dead King:

> 'We have cause to rejoice for the virtuous and praiseworthy life that his Majesty hath led – as also for his very good death. Let us take comfort by praising his prudence and goodness, and for the very great care he hath taken of his kingdom at the close of his life, having prayed God to defend it from the Popish faith, and to deliver it from the rule of his evil sisters. His Majesty hath well weighed an act of Parliament wherein it was already resolved that whosoever should acknowledge the Lady Mary or the Lady Elizabeth and receive them as heirs of the crown should be had for traitors, one of them having formerly been disobedient to his Majesty's father King Henry VIII, and also himself, concerning the true religion. Wherefore in no manner did His Grace wish that they should be his heirs – he being in every way able to disinherit them.'

By now Jane would certainly have guessed what was coming next. Describing herself as 'stupefied and troubled' she began to tremble. Then came the words she most feared to hear:

'His Majesty hath named Your Grace as the heir to the
crown of England. Your sisters will succeed you in the
case of your default of issue.'

Still the rasping voice went on, scarcely choosing to notice the
state of shock into which his words had thrown Lady Jane:

'This declaration hath been approved by all the Lords of
the Council, most of the peers and by all the judges of
the land, and all this confirmed and ratified by letters patent under the Great Seal of England. There is nothing
wanting but Your Grace's grateful acceptance of the high
estate which God Almighty, the sovereign and disposer
of all crowns and sceptres – never sufficiently to be
thanked by you for so great a mercy – hath advanced to
you.'

At this point the Duke turned to Jane, doubtless expecting some
grateful response, and spoke to her directly,

'Therefore you should cheerfully take upon you the name,
title and estates of Queen of England, France [England
still had possession of several French towns], and
Ireland.'

It was all too much. The grievous news of her cousin's death
and the even greater shock that the crown had been left to her
was more than the girl could sustain. The colour drained from
her cheeks as she swayed and fell to the floor in a dead faint. It
seemed that no one moved to help her. Moments later she came
round, and still those silent figures stood there watching her.
Terror overwhelmed her and she burst into tears: tears first of all
for Edward… 'so noble a prince', she managed to sob. Then
controlling herself as she had long learnt to do in her difficult
childhood, she spoke clearly and deliberately: 'The crown is not
my right, and pleaseth me not. The Lady Mary is the rightful
heir.'

This was not what the gathered nobility expected or wished to hear. 'Your grace doth wrong to yourself and to your house!' growled the angry Duke. Jane remained adamant. Her parents glared and reminded her of her duty of obedience, and her young husband, 'dazzled by so brilliant a destiny', thought it was time for him to take part and began to 'cajole, caress with feigned kisses', and flatter his frightened wife. What should she do? Stunned and silent she looked from one to the other. Would no one help her? Then kneeling down, she turned to the only one she could trust – to her God for direction in this desperate hour. What transpired in those moments as the girl knelt in prayer we may not know. She recognized that she had a duty of obedience to her parents, to the Privy Council and most of all to Edward VI, until so recently her King. Perhaps God gave her some inner assurance of his purposes behind all these perplexing events and his peace to her troubled spirit. Remaining on her knees she spoke calmly as if still in prayer:

'If what hath been given to me is lawfully mine, may thy divine Majesty grant me such grace that I may govern to thy glory and service, to the advantage of this realm.'

Once Lady Jane had seen her way as ordered by her God, she became controlled and strong. Allowing someone to help her from her knees she was led to the waiting throne and seated upon it. Then all present knelt before her one by one, kissed her hand and professed loyalty 'even to the death'.[2]

CHAPTER TWELVE
A COUNTERCLAIM

After the tumultuous events of the previous evening Jane must have been exhausted as she snatched a few hours' sleep on Sunday night, 9 July 1553, at Syon House, home of her new in-laws. Whether or not the full implications of all that had happened had yet dawned on her we do not know, but it would not be hard for her to see through the religious affirmations of some about her; men who were above all hungry for power and prestige.

The next morning the nation would be presented with its new Queen and Jane must be properly arrayed for the occasion. With the help of her faithful nurse Mistress Ellen, and probably her mother fussing around, Jane was carefully dressed in a magnificent gown of Tudor green with wide sleeves, interlaced with gold and embellished with rubies, emeralds and diamonds. With her long auburn hair neatly fitted under a white jewelled hood, she may have looked regal enough, but because of her petite figure it would not be easy for the people to see her. The only answer was to strap a pair of three-inch-high wooden clogs on to Jane's shoes to add to her height. Then came the long lonely journey up the Thames in the royal barge from Syon House to the Tower of London, where monarchs traditionally waited until their coronation.

Heralds were sent throughout London proclaiming both the death of the well-loved King Edward, and the ascendancy of 'Jane of Suffolk' to the throne. 'Jane who?' the people would have asked, for although she had been occasionally at court during the last four years, much of her time had been spent at Bradgate Park in Leicestershire. Few citizens of London would have known who she was. And what about the King's older sister, Mary, rightful heir to the throne according to Henry VIII's will? The stunned populace learned that Edward had changed the Act of Succession in the last month of his life, leaving his throne to his little-known cousin, Jane.

As the royal barge passed slowly up the river, crowds lined the bank to watch its progress, but they were not cheering – only a glum silence greeted the new Queen. Perhaps they were mourning the death of Edward, but the omens for the new reign were not good. Not that personal grudges were held against Jane herself for it was Northumberland who was held in utmost contempt by the people. Jane would be widely viewed merely as Northumberland's puppet, set up by him to retain his own hold on power and to rob them of their rightful Queen.

When the royal barge arrived at the Tower, the cannons boomed out their salute to greet the new Queen. Jane picked up her long skirts and stepped gingerly ashore. Slowly the rest of the royal party alighted, but few citizens of London had gathered around to watch her arrival. Even fewer cried out with any degree of enthusiasm, 'God save the Queen'. Baptista Spinola, a Genoese merchant, watched as Jane alighted and has left one of the best descriptions we have of her:

> 'This Jane is very short and thin, but prettily shaped and graceful. She has small features and a well made nose, the mouth flexible and the lips red. The eyebrows are arched and darker than her hair, which is nearly red. Her eyes are sparkling and reddish brown in colour. I stood so near her Grace that I noticed her colour was good but freckled. When she smiled she showed her teeth which are white and sharp. In all, a gracious and animated figure.'

He had other comments to make as well.

> 'She is now called Queen, but is not popular, for the hearts of the people are with Mary, the Spanish Queen's daughter,' and he added tellingly, 'This lady is very heretical and has never heard Mass, and some great people did not come into the procession for that reason.'

Lady Jane Grey

Few others besides Spinola bothered to chronicle Lady Jane's arrival at the Tower. Sir John Bridges, the Lieutenant of the Tower, together with the Marquess of Winchester, the Lord Treasurer, were there to greet the royal party. The Yeomen warders of the Tower, each with a shining axe upon his shoulder, lined the route. Guilford, Jane's husband, attended her with suitably low bows, while her mother, with as much grace as she could muster, carried her daughter's train. After a few moments Jane, her parents, husband, nobles and ladies-in-waiting, were all swallowed up within the precincts of the Tower, that ancient symbol of England's historic past.

The White Tower, the central keep of the Tower of London, had been built five hundred years earlier in the days of William the Conqueror. It housed the royal apartments and here Jane would remain until her coronation. Scarcely did she have time to take in her new environment before the Marquess of Winchester, who had disappeared for a few moments, reappeared carrying various jewels belonging to the Crown, and most significant of all – the Crown of England itself. Jane had probably never seen the crown close up before, nor gazed at the Black Prince's Ruby glowing in magnificent splendour, or seen the sparkling blue sapphire of Edward the Confessor, said to date from 1042. Awestruck, she gazed upon it. This crown, the symbol of monarchy, held an almost spiritual significance for a Tudor. Only God appointed kings and with their appointment came that newly-created and solemn responsibility to be Head of the Church.

The Marquess of Winchester had brought the crown so that Jane could try it on to see how well it suited her, and also to check if any adjustments were needed to make it fit her better. The suggestion appalled her and she refused to try it on. 'It had never been demanded by me, or by anyone in my name,' she recorded. 'Your grace may take it without fear,' said Winchester smoothly. In that sickening moment, as Jane stood looking at the crown, she felt a rush of despair and horror. Certainly the previous night, with the highest nobles of the land glowering down at her, she had accepted the fact that Edward had named her as his successor; there had been little alternative. Now the full meaning of all that had transpired became starkly clear, and Winchester's next words revealed a further element of the whole scheme that Northumberland had devised.

After pressing her to try on the crown, Winchester continued: 'And another shall be made to crown your husband withal'. Had she heard aright? A crown for Guilford? 'I, for my part,' she later confessed, 'heard truly with a troubled mind and with ill-will, even with infinite grief and displeasure of heart.' Guilford Dudley, her sixteen-year-old husband, to be crowned king of England? But he had not a drop of royal blood in his veins. It was all part of Northumberland's crafty plan to retain power and claim the throne for his family. Perhaps – Jane may have surmised wildly, for she had already suspected it – he intended to poison her and then Guilford would be king in his own right. Her predicament was dire. If Northumberland's scheme failed, she would be executed for high treason, the automatic penalty for any who interfered with the royal succession; if it succeeded, she could well die an even worse death than execution.

With all the verve that had become characteristic of Lady Jane, she declared to Guilford who was standing beside her, in a tone both firm and final, 'I will not have you crowned king.' And to back up her decision she explained that it could not be done without an Act of Parliament. Astonished at Jane's tone and the prospect of having his will crossed – a rare event in his life – Guilford exclaimed petulantly, 'I will be made king by you and by Act of Parliament!' But Jane was adamant. Nothing would make her change her mind. As Guilford burst into tears she could see that a family row of enormous magnitude was brewing and conceded, 'If the crown belongs to me [a comment that reveals her deep unease], I would be content to make my husband a duke.' Heedless of this compromise, Guilford ran from the room to fetch his mother. The Duchess of Northumberland soon returned together with her tearful son and berated Jane for such an insult. 'I will not be a duke. I will be King,' insisted Guilford. But seeing that words were useless, Jane's mother-in-law grabbed her offended son and marched him out of the room, declaring that she was taking him back to Syon House; and to Guilford she added, as a parting insult to Jane, 'You shall no longer sleep with her.' With quick reaction Jane ordered two of the noblemen who stood by to prevent the agitated pair from leaving for she could not afford such a public humiliation at that moment. The Duchess and her son had no option other than to obey.

Three letters were written in Jane's name and sent out under the signature of 'Jane the Queen' during the course of the next few days. Although probably composed on her behalf they demonstrate how seriously Lady Jane took the new responsibilities that had fallen to her. The first, written on 11 July, announced her accession to the crown and was addressed to the Marquess of Northampton, Katherine Parr's brother. The second, dated 16 July, demanded allegiance from various Justices of the Peace, and the third, written two days later, was addressed to Sir John Bridges, Lieutenant of the Tower.

While all this was going on an unwelcome letter reached London sent on 10 July, the very day that Jane had been proclaimed Queen. Written from Kenninghall in Norfolk, where Lady Mary was taking temporary refuge, it expressed Mary's dismay that she had not been told earlier of her brother's death, and demanded that her entitlement to the throne should be proclaimed throughout the capital. Such a letter was deeply disturbing. As it was read aloud to the party in the White Tower, both Jane's mother and her mother-in-law, who realized instantly the importance of such a development, reacted tearfully. Jane did not weep, but now she knew that her father-in-law's scheme could well collapse if the people should rise in support of Mary.

Although such information must have caused the fifteen-year-old deep apprehension, she was a practical young woman so said little but continued with the immediate matters of state that needed attention: sending out instructions to foreign ambassadors and attending Privy Council meetings. Only two days later, on

12 July, after Jane had been Queen for three days, the full extent of Mary's counterclaim began to filter through to the White Tower. As Mary began her slow advance towards London, the people had begun flocking to her cause. The Earls of Bath and Sussex, plus various other representatives of the nobility, were joining her triumphant march. Evidently Robert Dudley, son of the Duke of Northumberland, who had been commissioned to capture and hold Mary, had been ineffectual in his attempt to arrest her progress.

Lady Jane knew that if she was to be Queen her supporters would have to fight for her. Who would be best suited to rally support in her favour and stand most likelihood of success? The unanimous opinion of the nobles around her was that her own father, the Duke of Suffolk, would be the most obvious choice to lead a force against Mary and her supporters, for the Duke of Northumberland's unpopularity would make him less effectual on such a mission. At that moment Jane made her first and most serious mistake. Deeply suspicious of the devious Northumberland, she dreaded being left alone with him. Since her forced marriage to Guilford Dudley she had been showing signs of stress: her hair was beginning to fall out, as she later complained, and her skin had become inflamed. Surely these were signs that her new father-in-law was systematically poisoning her; or so Jane thought. No, she could not allow her own father to go; he must stay with her in the Tower. When the nobles showed their reluctance at such a change, Jane lost that self-control that had marked her since she had been declared Queen and burst into tears. She insisted that the Duke of Northumberland himself must go to meet the insurgents.

Hated and despised, Northumberland knew he could not command any popular support. His mere presence on the field of battle would be sufficient to deter many from joining Jane's cause. But with a tearful Queen on their hands and fear gnawing into the hearts of all who had vowed to remain faithful to Jane 'even to death', the other nobles persuaded John Dudley that he was indeed the man for the hour, and realizing this was the best option in the circumstances, he began to raise troops to fight his cause.

It was a two-fold mistake. With the intimidating presence of the Duke out of the Tower, those who had promised to support Jane would be able to slip away and declare their allegiance for Mary, should their undertaking become untenable. No one would be there to stop them. Northumberland himself was well able to see the folly of leaving Jane in the custody of men whom he could only half trust. But he had little alternative. Jane thanked him sincerely for his willingness to fight on her behalf. 'I will do what in me lies,' replied the Duke, but with a note of uncertainty in his words. Then pledging his willingness to offer up his life for his new Queen, John Dudley gathered his troops; yet before he set out he once again urged those who remained to act with honour and faithfulness towards Lady Jane. As he did so he acknowledged that she herself had not asked for the throne of England but had been 'rather by force placed thereon than by her own seeking and request'. Protestations of loyalty from his fellow Privy Council members present in the Tower gave Northumberland a measure of confidence in his mission as he set off 'to bring in the Lady Mary, captive or dead, like the rebel she is'. The Earl of Arundel even added, 'I am sorry not to go with your Grace. I could spend my blood even at your feet.'

Northumberland had not been gone long before he realized the enormity of the task awaiting him. Flanked by two of his sons and followed by his troops, he rode out of London on 14 July, his brilliant red cloak creating a show of bravado. But the crowds who saw him pass watched in silence. None raised a cheer, or wished him well in his dangerous enterprise. Northumberland's plan was to march towards Newmarket where he hoped to intercept Mary's progress but his advance was slow and all the time his men were defecting and joining the opposing ranks. In despair he sent an urgent message back to the Tower asking for reinforcements as town after town declared allegiance to the princess. Jane herself sent a request to the French king – who at that time was in friendly alliance with England – for 6000 troops to bolster her cause.

Four nobles remained in the Tower: Arundel, Pembroke, Cecil and Winchester, but they were becoming increasingly restive. Each had much to lose. If Mary were to succeed in her bid for the throne, they were the ones who would be declared guilty of high treason and end their days victim to the executioner's axe. Arundel, the last to proffer undying support to Northumberland, actually wrote to Mary warning her of the Duke's advance. He also had old scores to settle with Henry Grey, for it was Arundel's daughter that Henry had jilted in order to marry Frances many years earlier.

On Sunday 16 July, exactly a week after Jane had been informed of Edward's 'Devise' for the succession, Nicholas Ridley, Bishop of London, preached a rousing sermon at St Paul's Cross. He declared loyalty to his new Queen but was so booed, jeered and hissed at by the angry crowd, he could scarcely make his voice heard. Neither Mary nor Elizabeth, he declared, had any right to the throne, for both had been pronounced illegitimate and were therefore disqualified for the succession. Moreover, Mary, as a Roman Catholic, would fall under the influence of some Catholic prince, and both women might undermine the sovereignty of England by some foreign marriage alliance. The people, who held the Tudor blood-line in strong respect, were not troubled by such niceties as legal prohibitions; they felt deprived of their rightful queen. They 'murmured sore' at Ridley and refused to listen. Bishop Hugh Latimer also denounced the two princesses in equally stringent tones that day, adding that it would be better that they should die than the true religion be undermined.

On that same Sunday Northumberland reached Cambridge and here he attended a morning service. Dr Sandys, Vice-Chancellor of the university, preached a sermon supporting Jane's right to the throne, but with the Duke's dwindling forces and daily defections from his cause, he must have listened to such a sermon with an ever-growing scepticism. At last on 17 July he drew near to Bury St Edmunds, little more than thirty-five miles from Framlingham, north of Ipswich, where Mary and her army were presently encamped. Only a week earlier Jane had been declared Queen, but now her cause hung in the balance. County after county was declaring allegiance for Mary and her armed forces stood at 20,000 men. Worse news for the Duke was to follow as he learned that the men on the seven naval vessels docked in Yarmouth, ready to prevent Mary from escaping out of the country, had mutinied as they too had proclaimed her as their rightful Queen.

The nobles remaining in the White Tower knew they could not confer with one another in Jane's presence, and so, one by one, they slipped out, ostensibly on some royal errand, but with little intention of returning unless there was a significant change in developments. Jane herself, who had made little comment on the rumours that were daily increasing, soon realized that she could not trust her professed supporters and ordered the gates to be locked at seven o'clock each night and the keys to be brought to her. Pembroke and Winchester, who had both managed to escape, were ordered to return under armed escort.

By 18 July, despite all precautions, only three of the men who had first accompanied Jane to the Tower remained loyal to her: her own father, the Duke of Suffolk; Archbishop Thomas Cranmer; and Sir John Cheke, faithful friend and tutor of Edward VI. All the others, including Winchester, who had tried to thrust the crown on the new Queen, had gone. The Earl of Arundel had left on some pretext of raising extra support, whereas his real intention was to defect to Mary and to persuade as many of the Privy Council still loyal to Jane to do the same. Unskilled in political intrigue, Jane probably still trusted them and it is doubtful if she realized how precarious her situation had become. Instead she spent her time setting out the agenda for her reign: the primary consideration being the consolidation of the Reformation in both church order and in the nation as a whole.

Baynard Castle, London home of the wealthy Lord Herbert, the Earl of Pembroke – whose son had been married to Jane's younger sister – became the venue for the dissident members of the Privy Council who now declared the Duke of Northumberland himself to be a traitor to 'their sovereign Lady Mary'. A letter was constructed demanding the Duke's surrender and the

disbanding of his army. Receiving no answer from the embat-
tled Duke, Arundel, his erstwhile colleague, set off for Cambridge
to arrest him. But before doing so, he rode many miles out of
his way to Framlingham to offer his loyal obeisance to Mary.
Meanwhile Northumberland, finding his army reduced to a
pathetic remnant, retreated back to Cambridge where he made
desperate attempts to recruit a peasant army to fight his cause.
Unloved and disdained, he met with nothing but indifference or
insult.

Assured of the support of key men such as Arundel, Pembroke
and Winchester, the Privy Council now publicly proclaimed
Mary's triumph, and on 19 July announced throughout
London that the daughter of their former sovereign, Henry VIII,
was their new Queen. London went mad with joy, not so much
out of antipathy to Jane but rather to the Duke of Northumberland who was seen as the master schemer, depriving Mary of
her rightful throne. Cheers resounded through the capital,
bonfires were lit, bells rang from every church. One Italian
observer watched in blank amazement as the people 'ran hither
and thither, bonnets flew into the air, shouts rose higher than
the stars, fires were lit on all sides ... from a distance the earth
must have looked like Mount Etna'. Even many of the London
Protestants joined in, little realizing the significance of what they
were doing. The Earl of Pembroke emerged from his stately residence to throw money to the people, celebrating the success of
Mary's claim as much as anyone. He promptly declared his son's
marriage to Katherine Grey null and void and sent the bewildered girl home again.

The distant sound of cheering gradually penetrated the old
walls of the White Tower. Louder it grew and louder. Surely it
could not be the Duke of Northumberland returning in triumph,
bringing the captive Mary with him? But as the crescendo of joy
became ever stronger, ever wilder, the truth must have dawned
upon Jane: Mary had been proclaimed Queen of England.
Almost alone in her quiet apartment with only her faithful nurse,
Mistress Ellen, and her lady attendant, Mrs Tylney, still with her,
Jane would have heard another sound, much closer at hand –

footsteps ascending the old stone stairway up to the royal apartments.

Jane's father, the Duke of Suffolk, burst into the room where Jane sat under the royal canopy. 'You are no longer Queen', was his brusque message and with his own hands he began tearing down the canopy under which his daughter had been sitting. 'You must put off your royal robes and be content with a private life.' Jane's reply was totally characteristic of her: 'I much more willingly put them off than I put them on. Out of obedience to you and my mother I have grievously sinned. Now I willingly relinquish the crown.' Then she added, 'May I not go home?'

But Jane could not go home. Her father had every intention of abandoning his daughter to her fate. Once Mary arrived in London his own head would be far from secure and his mind was now set on trying to save his life. He determined to leave Jane in the Tower while he went out and ordered his men-at-arms to lay down their weapons. Then he declared as loudly as any 'Long live Queen Mary'. Returning to his home in Sheen, Jane's father, followed shortly afterward by her mother, hoped by suitable demonstrations of loyalty to escape implication in Northumberland's stratagem to make their daughter Queen. Even Jane's husband Guilford, and his mother the Duchess of Northumberland, were nowhere to be seen at that lonely moment.

Why, it might be asked, should the people of England rise in support of Mary in so spectacular a fashion causing even her closest supporters to call it a miracle? An immediate answer must lie in the public perception of the Duke of Northumberland. Despite the fact that his period in power had begun to rectify some of the economic ills of the country, he was widely blamed for many things; particularly for the overthrow of 'the Good Duke', Edward Seymour. His cunning ambition earned him contempt from high and low alike. Added to this a strong sense of the legality of Mary's claim to the throne was a major factor, together with veneration for the memory and wishes of Henry VIII. At that moment the question of religion did not seem to have been a central issue. Basically it was a revolt of the people against the central government as represented by the Duke of Northumberland. Men and women of convinced evangelical persuasion also added their support for Mary. Her insistence on the celebration of Mass in private was generally known, but the depth of her antipathy to evangelical doctrine was less obvious. At worst she might wish to restore the religious settlement to the way it had been left by Henry VIII at his death, but even those close to Mary were unaware of her hidden agenda to bring her country back under the domination of the pope.

'I am glad I am no longer Queen,' said Jane simply to her attendants when she returned to her private apartments and reported her father's announcement. Helping the girl to take off her royal robes, Mistress Ellen and Mrs Tylney wept bitterly as they listened to her calm words. They guessed, even if Jane did not, that she might never leave the Tower again.

CHAPTER THIRTEEN
DEFENCELESS AND ALONE

Forsaken by all except his sons and a handful of loyal men, the Duke of Northumberland was still in Cambridge when he heard the news that he most dreaded: London had declared allegiance for Mary. As the Duke paced about in the grounds of King's College on the morning of 19 July 1553 the university sergeant-at-arms drew near with orders to arrest him. Confronted by a man wild with rage and despair, the sergeant quickly decided against such a course of action, and the Duke strode out into the market place where a declaration of Lady Jane's accession to the throne had been pasted up. Ripping it down with his own hands, he filled his velvet cap with gold coins and waved it in the air; and as the people scrambled to pick up the money, he shouted 'Long live Queen Mary!' But by this time he was in a state of near hysteria and burst out laughing while the tears streamed down his cheeks.

After attending a morning service at Great St Mary's, he ordered Dr Sandys to conclude with a celebration of the Mass – a sad comment on the Duke's lack of any true spiritual convictions for it was he who had urged the progress of the Reformation ever onward during Edward's reign. As he was preparing to return to Bury St Edmunds from where he planned to make his escape, an unwelcome visitor hammered on the door of his lodging. There confronting him was the Earl of Arundel – the man who had undertaken to stand by him to the death. Northumberland could do little else than fall on his knees and beg for clemency. But it was in vain. As we have seen, he had been responsible for imprisoning Arundel for a full year because of his support for the former Protector. Now was the time for revenge. As he shackled the Duke of Northumberland, Arundel replied coldly, 'You should have sought for mercy sooner, my lord.'

Stripped of his sword and humiliated, the man who had held all England in an iron grip was shut up in his room in Cambridge, and kept securely guarded for some days while Arundel awaited further instructions from London. Five days later the prisoner, together with his sons, made their slow progress to London. As the party arrived the scenes were even more extraordinary than they had been the previous week, when Mary's accession to the throne had been proclaimed. Now the people were intent on murdering the hapless Duke. 'Death to the traitor! Death to the traitor!' yelled the crowd, as they attempted to lunge forward and drag him from his horse. Rotten eggs, stones; any missile that lay near to hand was thrown at the man who was universally hated. Only by threatening the crowd with their long pikes were the guards able to command any restraint.

Simon Renard, the Spanish ambassador who would become special adviser to Mary, left an eyewitness account. 'Armed men were posted all along the streets to prevent the people, greatly excited as they were, from falling on the Duke.' Hatless, and stripped of his scarlet cloak, possibly to make him less conspicuous to the angry crowd, or even an added insult devised by Arundel, he rode on through the London streets. 'He wished to move the people and his friends to pity,' reported Renard, 'but notwithstanding his courtesy the people cried out upon him. A dreadful sight, a strange mutation.'

At last the abject party that comprised the Duke, two of his sons and other close supporters reached the Tower of London, scene of his recent triumphs. But now he entered not as the all-powerful figure of two weeks earlier but as a pathetic, beaten man. As so often happens, the bully had become the coward. The seeds of his downfall can be traced to his own domineering and underhanded behaviour. The historian G. M. Trevelyan describes the Dudley era of English history as 'the high water mark of corruption and greed', and adds this telling description of the man himself:

'People of all religions soon recognised that Dudley rang
as false on the counter as one of the bad coins issued by
his government... In warfare and in political intrigue he
had both skill and courage, but these availed little to save
a man without statesmanship whom all detested.'

It must be added, however, that the historical perception of the
Duke of Northumberland has been over-harsh. It was he who
had succeeded, where Edward Seymour had failed, in bringing
the war with France to an end. He had abandoned the attempt
to subjugate Scotland. Both of these enterprises had emptied
the nation's coffers and had contributed to the alarming inflation during Edward's reign.

Together with the Duchess of Northumberland and all his
sons apart from Guilford, the Duke was imprisoned in the
Beauchamp Tower – near enough the White Tower to emphasize to him the irony of his situation. Here too were imprisoned
a number of others whom Mary considered culpable in the plot
to place Lady Jane on the throne – innocent men among them.
Bishop Nicholas Ridley was there, for he had preached the
sermon denouncing Mary and proclaiming Jane's legitimate right
to the throne; so too was Lord Chief Justice Montague, the old
lawyer with seventeen children who had been so reluctant to
sign King Edward's 'Devise'. Sir John Cheke, Edward's tutor,
now Secretary of State, and Dr Sandys of Cambridge also found
themselves arraigned for supporting Jane, and were in the
Beauchamp Tower.

Immediately adjacent to the Beauchamp Tower stood the
residence of Master Partridge, 'Gentleman Gaoler of the Tower',
a high sounding title that played down his unpleasant occupation as a prison warder, a post he held under the Lieutenant of
the Tower, Sir John Bridges. Partridge's half-timbered house
overlooked Tower Green, a sinister spot where executions of
high-profile prisoners such as Anne Boleyn, mother of Elizabeth, and Catherine Howard, fourth wife of Henry VIII, had
been carried out. Here it was that Jane was taken, together with

her two lady attendants, a page boy and also accompanied by Lady Throckmorton, wife of Sir Nicholas, a staunch upholder of the Reformation. Guilford had been removed to the Beauchamp Tower to join the rest of his family.

The Lord Treasurer, the Marquess of Winchester, the very one who had urged Jane to wear the crown of England without fear, was now deputed to order her to make a formal renunciation of the crown, and also to strip the girl of every vestige of royalty: her jewels, mufflers, hats, furs and even family portraits. Unable to find certain missing jewels, he robbed her of virtually all her personal possessions of any value. All that was left to Jane, and probably all that she wanted at this grievous time, was her Greek New Testament, a small book of prayers and meditations,[1] and her writing materials. She was forbidden to have any communication with Guilford, even though he was near at hand, and was left with scarcely enough money to cover the fee she had to pay to the gaoler for her board.[2]

Jane's parents, meantime, were quietly settled back at their family home in Sheen, maintaining a judicious and low-key existence; but not for long. Mary was under no illusions as to the part the Duke of Suffolk had played in the attempt to deprive her of what she regarded as her rightful throne. Within ten days he too was arrested and brought to the Tower. Before his arrest Frances Grey had made a personal approach to the new Queen to plead her husband's cause – the two women were cousins and had once been on friendly terms, with the Grey family having been guests in Mary's palatial homes. The Duke of Northumberland had been trying to poison them all, as he had done her dying brother, Frances told the Queen. Whether or not Mary believed her story, we are not told – she certainly asked what proof Frances had for this – but even so ordered Henry Grey's release after only three days in the Tower. Doubtless she also stipulated that a careful watch should be kept upon him. It appears that neither Jane's father nor her mother did much, if anything, to help their daughter, innocent victim of their own boundless ambition. Nor did they attempt to visit her;

all they cared for was to extricate themselves from any blame, and to emphasize their loyalty to Mary.

The martyrologist, John Foxe, records a prayer offered by Lady Jane, 'in the time of her trouble', and certainly these early days of her imprisonment, the dupe of unscrupulous men and forsaken by those who should have supported her, were indeed such a time:

> 'Let it seem good to thy fatherly goodness to deliver me, sorrowful wretch (for whom thy Son Christ shed his precious blood on the cross) out of this miserable captivity and bondage wherein I am now. How long wilt thou be absent? for ever? O Lord, hast thou forgotten to be gracious, and hast thou shut up thy loving-kindness in displeasure? Shall I despair of thy mercy, O God? Far be that from me. I am thy workmanship created in Christ Jesus. Give me grace therefore to tarry thy leisure ... only in the mean time, arm me, I beseech thee, with thy armour that I may stand fast ... that I may reserve myself wholly to thy will...'

In addition to her prayers, Jane took the practical step of writing a long letter to Mary, carefully explaining the circumstances that had led her to adopt the title of Queen.

On 3 August 1553 Mary had made her triumphal progress into the capital. To the blast of trumpets, the thirty-nine-year-old elder daughter of Henry VIII, arrayed in a gown of purple velvet – Mary always compensated for what she lacked in personal beauty by extravagant clothing – made her ceremonial way through Aldgate and towards the White Tower. Many wept for joy and others cried out until they were hoarse, 'God bless your Grace!' By her side rode Elizabeth, who had wisely remained quietly at her Hatfield Palace during these tumultuous days, and was now temporarily reconciled to her older sister. Probably happier than she had ever been in her cheerless life, Mary was in a benign frame of mind and Jane had certainly chosen a timely occasion for her letter.

The original of Jane's long letter has disappeared, only a translation into Italian, retranslated into English, remains. For a fifteen-year-old, Jane had an extraordinary facility with her pen, and now she told Mary the whole sad story of her forced marriage, even after she was already betrothed to another, and of the duplicity with which the crown had been foisted upon her. 'No one can ever say that I sought it or was pleased with it,' she wrote. Describing the adulation heaped on her by Dudley, Arundel and others, she wrote of how 'with unwont'd caresses and pleasantness, [they] did me such reverence as was not at all suitable to my state'. So even though she recognized that she deserved 'heavy punishment', she pointed out that 'the error imputed to me has not been altogether caused by myself'. Apologizing humbly for her part in the circumstances, she continued in a long and complicated sentence,

'Although my fault be such that but for the goodness and clemency of the Queen, I can have no hope of pardon nor in finding forgiveness, having given ear to those who at that time appeared to be wise, and now having shown themselves to be contrary, and having such shameful boldness tried to give to others what was not theirs ... nevertheless I trust in God that as I now know and confess my want of prudence, I can still conceive hope of your infinite clemency.'

Mary had known Jane from the days when the nine-year-old had lived with the family during Katherine Parr's life. She had been fond of the child and sent her gifts from time to time. Jane's strong adherence to the 'New Religion' had annoyed Mary, but perhaps there was hope of bringing her to change her mind. She would have seethed with anger against Northumberland as Jane continued,

'The Duke was the first to persuade King Edward to make me his heir... I know for certain that twice during this time poison was given to me, first in the house of the Duchess

of Northumberland and afterwards here in the Tower...[3]
All these things I have wished to say, to the witness of my
innocence and the disburdening of my conscience.'

Such a letter weighed strongly with Mary and she was determined that she should not begin her reign with exacting
punishment on all who had supported Jane, nor on Jane
herself whom she saw as the victim of an ill-conceived plot. To
forgive her Councillors, all twenty-five of whom had signed
papers supporting Jane, was one thing, but to trust them was
another. Mary Tudor was astute enough to know that if they
could swap allegiance so easily, and many of them their religion
too, then they could as easily turn against her once more. Mary
had little love for the English and throughout her twisted and
deprived childhood she had turned to her mother's country,
Spain, for allegiance and to her mother's staunch Catholicism
for support. Although she could not rule the country without
the aid of the Council, it was to Simon Renard, the Spanish
ambassador, that she now turned for advice.

Renard had inveigled his way into Mary's confidence and as
her personal advisor he influenced her policies during 1553 and
1554. Still in a benevolent mood, Mary intimated to Renard
that she intended to pardon the Duke of Northumberland. Her
uncle, Charles V, German Emperor, King of Spain and the Netherlands, had written cautioning her against dealing harshly with
her enemies, but Renard was horrified at the suggestion of
pardon for the Duke and urged that Northumberland's trial and
execution should take place as soon as it could be arranged.
And as for 'Jane of Suffolk' both she and her husband should
be put to death, Renard insisted. But Mary sprang to Jane's
defence, telling him that three days before Jane had been
proclaimed as Queen, she had known nothing of it. 'My
conscience will not permit me to have her put to death,' she
affirmed. Nor would she recognize Jane's marriage to Guilford
to be valid, for 'she was previously betrothed'. Renard could
see that at present Mary was not willing for Jane to be executed,

but his ultimate aim was the annihilation of the whole Suffolk family, for he guessed that while Jane lived there would always be those who might try to put her on the throne once more.

As yet Mary kept secret her agenda to bring her country back to Rome and to stamp out the Protestant faith among her people. A statement read out on her behalf declared,

> 'She meaneth graciously not to compel or constrain other men's consciences otherwise than God shall (as she trusteth) put in their hearts a persuasion of the truth that she is in by the opening of his Word unto them by godly, virtuous and learned preachers.'

So she said, but there was also a clear hint that she hoped her people would naturally and gladly flock back to the Roman Church – a fact that shows how out of touch she was with the way that Reformation truth had gripped the hearts of sections of her nation.

In line with her policy of clemency wherever possible, Mary ordered the release of the Duchess of Northumberland, but when the Duchess ventured to approach Mary to plead on behalf of her husband and sons, she met with a stony response. Mary refused to see the wife of the one who had systematically insulted her and attempted to rob her of her crown. The trial of the Duke, his sons and others deemed to be guilty of high treason was arranged for 18 August, exactly one month after Mary had been declared Queen.

A pitiable and predictable occasion, the trial held one surprising element. Westminster Hall was redecorated for the proceedings, and the Catholic octogenarian, Thomas Howard, Duke of Norfolk, newly released from prison where he had languished since the death of Henry VIII, presided as judge over the trial. The axe-man led the way carrying his axe with its blade pointing away from the prisoners, then following behind him came all the Councillors, men who were once terrified of the Duke, but now sat in judgement over him. Although the Duke put up a spirited defence of his actions, insisting that all had been done under the authority of the Great Seal of England, he was found guilty. Slowly the axe-man turned the blade of his axe towards him, symbolizing guilt. Sentence was passed that he should be hung, drawn and quartered, the degrading death reserved for crime against the State. Accepting his sentence the Duke begged that he might be beheaded instead, that his family might be treated leniently, and, to the surprise of all, asked for time, saying that he now wished to be reconciled to the Church of Rome – an astonishing request in view of the harsh Protestant stance that he had adopted for many years. Clearly he hoped that by some outside chance such a turnabout might earn him a reprieve from his Catholic Queen.

CHAPTER FOURTEEN

A PRISONER OF THE CROWN

The Duke of Northumberland was allowed a twenty-four-hour reprieve in order to confess his apostasy and be reconciled to the Catholic Church. Calling for Stephen Gardiner, Bishop of Winchester, whom Mary had now released from prison, Northumberland made his confessions. Gardiner was the staunch Catholic bishop who had engineered the plot against Katherine Parr, and had been responsible for the torture and death of Anne Askew, Katherine's lady-in-waiting. Northumberland still clung to the outside chance that if he showed himself sufficiently penitent there might yet be clemency for him: 'I would do penance all the days of my life, if it were but in a mouse hole. Is there no hope of mercy?' he asked forlornly. Gardiner confirmed the greatness of his offence and said, 'I think you must die.' The weeping and distraught Duke then made a miserable admission: 'I can have no faith but yours. I never was of any other, indeed. I complied in King Edward's days only out of ambition, for which I pray God forgive me.'

The Queen momentarily hesitated at this abject confession, but with Simon Renard at her side to strengthen her nerve, she signed the death warrant. Still the Duke tried again. When he heard that the scaffold was being erected on Tower Hill, he wrote to his one-time associate, the Earl of Arundel, now basking in Mary's favour: 'Alas, my good lord, is my crime so heinous? A living dog is better than a dead lion. O, if it would please her good Grace to give me life, yea, but the life of a dog, if I might but live and kiss her feet...' Although such a pathetic appeal resulted in a further day or two granted to the Duke to make his peace with God, it was of no ultimate avail. On 22 August the Duke attended High Mass at the chapel of St Peter-ad-Vincula, within the Tower complex. Jane, who was standing at the window of the gaoler's house, watched him cross the Green. She commented wryly, 'I pray God that I, nor no friend of mine, die so.'

As he received the sacrament the Duke declared his total renunciation of the truths he had formerly espoused so rigorously, asserting his belief in the Catholic doctrine of transubstantiation. The next day he faced the scaffold initially with a degree of courage, assuring all of his forgiveness and taking an emotional farewell of his five sons. Only his eldest son, the Earl of Warwick, embraced the Catholic faith with his father; the other four, including Guilford, remained true to the evangelical beliefs their father had once upheld. Standing alone on that bitter scaffold the Duke addressed the thousands who had come to watch him die. Mysteriously he hinted that he himself 'had been seduced by others' to change the Succession and to name Jane as Queen rather than Mary. He declined to say who the 'others' might be, leaving posterity to indulge in guesses. To underline his re-conversion to the Catholic faith, he had stinging words to say about 'seditious preachers' who taught the people 'new doctrines':

'And one thinge more, good people, I haue to saye vnto you, whiche I am chiefly moved to do for discharge of my conscience, & that is to warne you and exhorte you to beware of these seditiouse preachers, and teachers of newe doctryne, which pretende to preache Gods worde, but in very deede they preache theyr owne phansies, who were neuer able to explicate themselues ... they open the boke, but they cannot shut it agayne. Take hede how you enter into straunge opinions or newe doctryne, whiche hath done no smal hurt in this realme, and hath iustlye procured the ire and wrath of God vpon vs.'

As the Duke had injured the true evangelical cause by his harsh, repressive and over-hasty determination to reform the church, so he further injured it in his death. In the cynical words of one bystander, 'He edified the people more than if all the Catholics

in the land had preached for ten years.' Many doubtful supporters of the 'New Religion' decided it was more expedient to return
to the safety of the 'Old'. But John Dudley's end was pitiable.
As the man who had terrorized the people, he was terrorized
himself by the ghastly approach of death. A chronicler of the
sad event wrote of the jumble of prayers and Hail Marys with
which he met his fate. 'He smote his hands together, as [if] to
say "This must be" and cast himself upon the block.' And so he
died. The Duke was buried in the chapel of St Peter-ad-Vincula,
side by side with none other than Edward Seymour, Duke of
Somerset, whose downfall he had helped to engineer.

Meanwhile his daughter-in-law, Lady Jane Dudley, remained
a prisoner of the crown. Lady Throckmorton, who had initially
attended Jane when she was first imprisoned, had left the Tower,
and Jane had only the company of two lady attendants, Mrs
Tylney and a Mrs Jacob, and of course her nurse, Mistress Ellen.
In addition a page boy was there to undertake more menial
tasks that Jane might require. She had her writing equipment
and one or two books. A fascinating contemporary document is
extant written in the form of a diary or journal probably by a
Rowland Lea who was an official of the royal mint and had
living accommodation in the Tower. In it Lea gives a graphic
picture of Lady Jane's life as a prisoner, referring to incidents
which took place at the end of August 1553, a week after the
execution of the Duke of Northumberland. Entitled *The Chronicle of Queen Jane and the First Two Years of Queen Mary,*[1] some
of the pencil-written account is now illegible, but a transcript
was published in 1850 and from this we draw some interesting
details of the conditions under which the fifteen-year-old was
being held.

It would seem that Jane's circumstances were now better than
at first. On the occasion described by Lea, she had decided to
take a meal with the gaoler and his wife, attended by her page
and one of her ladies – a privilege accorded to her if she should
so wish. Apparently granted a considerable degree of respect,
Jane was seated 'at the board's end' – the place of honour –

when an unexpected visitor entered the room. The visitor, probably none other than the chronicler of this anecdote, immediately
doffed his cap, a gesture that appears to have been a sign of
respect expected by and extended to the nobility alone. He had
not imagined that he would find Lady Jane in the company of
his friends, Partridge and his wife, and recorded that Jane had
immediately 'commanded Partridge and me to put on our caps',
and with remarkable poise had welcomed the newcomer and
had drunk his health.

Opening the conversation with the visitor, Jane commented,
'The Queen's majesty is a merciful princess. I beseech God she
may long continue and send his bountiful grace upon her.' She
was in a bright frame of mind that day for it had just filtered
through to her that, although she and Guilford must stand trial,
they were unlikely to face the death penalty for their part in the
events of recent weeks. Cut off from all the affairs of state, and
in particular from the traumatic events of recent days, Jane was
naturally eager to know what had been taking place. She had
heard that the evangelical preacher, John Rogers, had preached
at St Paul's Cross on 6 August, setting forth 'such true doctrine
that he and others had there taught in King Edward's days' – a
sermon that would eventually seal his fate. But who had
preached at St Paul's Cross the following Sunday, Jane wanted
to know? She was not surprised to learn that it was Gilbert
Bourne, one of Mary's own chaplains. Without doubt the visitor
would have told Jane of the violent reaction of the crowd to
Bourne's address with its return to Catholic teaching – repudiated by many of his listeners. There had been 'a great uproar
and shouting at his sermon', with cries of 'Kill him, kill him,'
coming from the incensed crowd.

'I pray you, have they Mass in London?' was Jane's next
question as she continued plying the newcomer with question
after question. Not surprisingly the conversation soon turned to
the apparent 'conversion' of the Duke of Northumberland back
to Catholicism (a thing which Jane considered 'so strange'), and
then to his execution. 'Perchance he hoped thereby to have his

pardon,' someone suggested. That was too much for Jane. All the pent-up anger, distress and pain of recent days came out in a torrent:

> 'Pardon? Woe worth him! He hath brought me and our stock in [to] most miserable calamity and misery by his exceeding ambition. But for the answering that he hoped for life by turning, though other men be of that opinion, I utterly am not; for what man is there living, I pray you, although he had been innocent, that would hope of life in that case; being in the field against the Queen in person as general; and after his taking [capture] so hated and evil spoken of by the commons? And at his coming into prison so wondered at [despised] as the like was never heard by any man's time. Who was judge that he should hope for pardon, whose life was odious to all men?'

No, in Jane's eyes the Duke had deserved all that he had received; but to her the worst of all was that he should renege on his faith in a pathetic hope of saving his head. She was now in full flow of invective and disdain:

> 'But what will ye more? Like his life was wicked and full of dissimulation, so was his end thereafter. I pray God, I, nor no friend of mine, die so. Should I who am young and in my few years, forsake my faith for the love of life? Nay, God forbid! Much more he should not, whose fatal course, although he had lived his just number of years, could not have long continued. Life is sweet, it appeared, so he might have lived in chains to have had his life… But God be merciful to us, for he sayeth, "Whoso denieth him before men, he will not know him in his Father's kingdom."'

Such a robust outburst reveals the character of Lady Jane to a remarkable degree. The picture of her 'rare and incomparable perfections', as described by one early writer, or as the gentle and timid maid beloved by Victorian authors, is far from the truth. Here was a true Tudor, strong, opinionated and indignant; but, more importantly, the strength of her reaction was kindled by a deep attachment to the faith of the gospel – an attachment which would be tested to the utmost in the days that lay ahead. Her indignation lay also in her total abhorrence of the Duke of Northumberland. Not only had his scheming stratagems brought ruin on her family, but even worse, he had sold his apparent faith in an attempt to secure a few more years of life. Had Jane been older she might have had a small shred of compassion for the unhappy man, but as a wronged fifteen-year-old she had nothing but disgust.

The conditions under which Lady Jane and her young husband, Lord Guilford Dudley, were being kept were now eased. After a month of close confinement Jane was allowed to take short walks around the precincts of the Tower. She was also allowed to meet Guilford, and the two young people, thrown together by the political manoeuvrings of their respective families, had an opportunity to learn to know one another away from the pressure of the hectic days following their marriage. Together they would walk around the grounds. There is some tradition that a degree of friendship and understanding began to develop between them; this is mainly based on the fact that the word 'JANE' was later found elaborately carved on the wall of Guilford's cell. His mother also bore the name 'Jane' and it could have been in honour of her that Guilford had carved the name – although the likelihood remains that it was indeed an inscription to his young wife.

With Simon Renard in constant attendance on the new Queen, the case of Lady Jane, Guilford and his two older brothers, Ambrose and Henry, was constantly brought to her attention. They must die, Renard insisted, if she were to enjoy her reign in peace, and particularly 'Jane of Suffolk' who had actually usurped the crown of England. At last, on 19 September, Mary could postpone Jane's trial no longer and agreed that these high-risk prisoners should shortly appear before Chief Justice Morgan and, if found guilty, face the death sentence.

The name 'JANE' was carved on the wall of Guilford's cell.
(From an original photograph by Lara E. Eakins
and used with her kind permission.)

Apart from this decision, Mary had little time to attend to the fate of her prisoners. First there was her coronation on 1 October, conducted with all the usual glitter and pageantry of such occasions. Dressed in purple denoting royalty, Mary's thin careworn frame looked almost attractive. Elizabeth, tall, youthful and dressed in white, was at her side; there was even a place for Jane's sister Katherine at the celebrations and for her mother, for Frances Grey was steadily winning her way back into favour at court.

Four days later Mary's first parliament met and not unexpectedly passed many far-reaching Acts. First, by the Act of Restitution, the divorce between Mary's mother, Katherine of Aragon, and Henry VIII was repealed and therefore all question of Mary's illegitimacy barring her becoming Queen was removed. Though demonstrating its unhappiness by a significant degree of reluctance, Parliament went on to undo all the church reforms of Edward's reign. Clergy were once more forbidden to marry, images were no longer to be banned from places of worship, and the confessional reinstated. The Act of Uniformity was annulled, laws against the celebration of the Mass repealed, and most sweeping of all, the Prayer Book of 1552 declared illegal. If Mary thought, however, that the ease with which she had gained her crown meant that the nation was anxious to repudiate Reformation truths, she soon learnt that this was not the case. Parliament had only consented to these measures after 'marvellous dispute'. Mary found the concept introduced in her father's reign, of the monarch as Supreme Head of the Church, highly distasteful and struggled to have it repealed to prepare the way for a full return to Rome. But here she met even stronger opposition. Few Englishmen wanted the pope once more to have a powerful voice in the country's affairs.

A further evidence of Mary's longer-term plans was to be seen in the removal of evangelical bishops such as John Hooper of Gloucester and Miles Coverdale of Exeter from their positions, substituting instead men of Catholic persuasion in the vacant bishoprics. Any perceptive observer would now have had evidence enough of the Queen's intentions for her country, even if formerly he had been more optimistic about her religious programme.

Another major question was also occupying the mind of Queen Mary – the vexed question of her own marriage. If Mary had a hidden agenda to bring England back under the dominion of Rome, Simon Renard the Spanish ambassador had another agenda of his own. Anxious to ally England with the imperial might of Spain against Henri II of France (the enemy of Charles V), Renard was pressing the suggestion of a marriage between Mary and Philip of Spain, the twenty-six-year-old son of Charles V. Mary at thirty-nine, prematurely aged and suffering indifferent health, was hardly an attractive proposition for the dashing young prince, but political alliances were the dominant factor in royal marriages. The idea of an unmarried queen in the sixteenth century was remote from the minds of the people – Mary must have a husband; but no Englishman would have favoured a Spaniard for such a position. England might then become a mere vassal state of Spain. For Mary to pursue such a marriage proposition would be the quickest way to ensure that the initial euphoria over her accession to the throne would evaporate.

During the month of October 1553 little changed in Jane's prison circumstances. Her sixteenth birthday came and went with few to celebrate it. Former prisoners were released, for one of Mary's first acts had been to pardon such powerful Catholics as Edmund Bonner, now restored as Bishop of London, Cuthbert Tunstall, Bishop of Durham, and as we have noted, Stephen Gardiner, Bishop of Winchester. New prisoners took their place and Jane would have heard that Archbishop Thomas Cranmer had joined other evangelical men already in the Tower; these included John Rogers, Nicholas Ridley and Hugh Latimer. Not only had Cranmer supported Jane's claim to the throne and sent a personal contingent of men to help Northumberland to capture Mary, but he had recently written (probably initially for private distribution) a Declaration against the Mass. When it was publicly displayed and spread around, he remained unapologetic for his views, nor would he retract his statements, a circumstance which led to his immediate incarceration. Cranmer would occupy the very room in the Beauchamp Tower so recently used by the Duke of Northumberland.

The surest method for any prisoner to gain his release was to renege on his declared faith and embrace the 'Old Religion' once more, attend Mass and publicly declare the errors of his former views. The Earl of Huntingdon was one who discovered that this was the quickest route to freedom, and in consequence was only in the Tower little more than a month. Following the declared apostasy of the Duke of Northumberland, many other members of the Privy Council also decided that it would be politically expedient to follow his example: men of the ilk of Arundel, Winchester and Pembroke, all prominent one-time supporters of the evangelical cause. Lady Jane had nothing but the utmost scorn for such men. The Duke had been executed before she had any opportunity of expressing her contempt for his cowardice, but a lengthy letter is extant, written by Jane to

Dr Harding, a former chaplain, supposedly an evangelical, who had once served her parents at Bradgate Manor, but had now returned to the Catholic fold.

Dr Harding may well have combined his duties as chaplain with that of tutor to Jane and her sisters. Some who have written accounts of the life of Lady Jane have felt a degree of embarrassment in the face of this letter written to one whom she had once respected, but now could only despise. One writer dismisses the letter as a fake. 'Can [such expressions] have issued from the mind or pen of an amiable young female? We think not,' writes George Howard in 1822. 'How could the girl, so often depicted as gentle and demure in character, write with such alarming scorn and invective?' others have asked. Insults aimed at the unstable chaplain follow one upon another like bullets from an automatic rifle:

> 'I cannot but marvel at thee and lament thy case, which seemed sometime to be a lively member of Christ, but now the deformed imp of the devil; sometime the beautiful temple of God, but now the filthy and stinking kennel of Satan; sometime the unspotted spouse of Christ, but now the unashamed paramour of antichrist; sometime my faithful brother, but now a stranger and an apostate; sometime a stout Christian soldier, but now a cowardly runaway.'

One explanation lies in Jane's circumstances. She had been deprived of her liberty, forsaken by her parents and tricked into accepting the crown by one who had also forced her into a marriage even though she was already engaged to another. Added to this, she was appalled by the ease with which the Duke and many others had jettisoned all their religious professions. Now Jane was venting her repressed feelings of indignation, bewilderment and betrayal on the head of one individual who personified much that she deprecated. Perhaps she thought that if she wrote strongly enough she might shock

Dr Harding into reconsidering the results of apostasy. Jane regarded his offence as even more odious than that of the politicians who changed religious allegiance to serve ambition or secure their fortunes. Harding had taught others the Word of God and his defection from the faith could cause many to stumble. As she continued to heap scornful words on her father's erstwhile chaplain with question after question, she also revealed her own grasp of biblical truth, astonishing for a girl of her age, together with her unusual ability to express herself and the depth of her spiritual convictions:

> 'Wilt thou resist thy Maker that fashioned thee and framed thee? Wilt thou now forsake him who called thee to be an ambassador and messenger of his eternal word? Darest thou deliver up thyself to another, being not thine own but his? Wilt thou refuse the true God, and worship the invention of man, the golden calf, the whore of Babylon, the Romish religion, the most wicked Mass? Wilt thou take it upon thee to offer up any other sacrifice unto God for our sins, considering that Christ offered up himself, as Paul saith, upon the cross, a lively sacrifice once for all?'

Jane ends her lengthy diatribe on a softer note.

> 'Certainly the Day of Judgement is approaching and the end of the apostate is fearsome, but there is still hope: Christ … now stretcheth out his arms to receive you, ready to fall upon your neck and kiss you.'

She concludes with a couplet to encourage her correspondent back into the true faith of the gospel:

> 'Be constant, be constant, fear not for any pain:
> Christ hath redeemed thee and heaven is thy gain.'

What effect such a letter had upon Dr Harding we cannot tell. But the fact that it has come down to posterity is perhaps an indication that the recipient did not discard it in anger but valued and preserved it. Certainly her own contemporaries did not regard the letter as strange or even offensive. It would later be circulated as a pamphlet and then included in John Foxe's *Book of Martyrs* – hugely popular reading material for many generations to come.

At last the date fixed for the trial arrived. On 13 November the Guildhall was prepared for the occasion and Chief Justice Richard Morgan was appointed to judge the prisoners arraigned before him. These included Archbishop Thomas Cranmer, Lady Jane, her husband Guilford, and Guilford's two older brothers, Ambrose and Henry. The party left the Tower by barge to travel up the river as far as the Guildhall. Leading the way from the riverside to the Guildhall went the axe-man with the blade of his axe pointing away from the prisoners. Next came the Archbishop walking slowly and with dignity. The route was lined by four hundred halberdiers, ensuring that no member of the public was allowed to approach the prisoners, and each member of the abject party was accompanied by guards.

Following the Archbishop and walking on her own came Lady Jane. Now that Mary was secure on her throne the curious citizens of London strained to catch a glimpse of the prisoners as they passed, for there was considerable public interest in the girl who had been proclaimed Queen for a few short days. Dressed entirely in black, her long velvet gown formed a sharp contrast to her auburn hair, young freckled face and wide, clear eyes. With a black satin hood, also trimmed in black, and her small black prayer book hanging from her waist, Jane was reading from a book of meditations and prayers as she walked along. She must have presented a stark picture, as bleak as her own circumstances. Behind her walked two of her lady attendants and next came the tall, fair, boyish-looking form of Guilford, followed by his brothers.

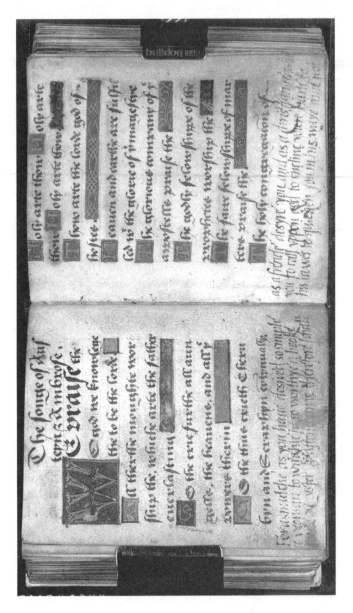

Lady Jane Grey's prayer book
(by kind permission of the British Library)

The proceedings were brief. First Judge Morgan read out the indictments against the accused, charging them with trying to annexe the crown from the rightful heir to the throne, to which Lady Jane and the Dudley brothers all pleaded guilty. Cranmer alone pleaded 'not guilty' at first, maintaining that he had acted in accordance with the dictates of the previous sovereign, until he too changed his plea. Then the Judge pronounced sentence: the young men would all face the ultimate penalty and be 'hung, drawn and quartered'. As for Lady Jane, she would die either by being burnt alive on Tower Hill or beheaded, as the Queen saw fit. At some point, perhaps as he was pronouncing sentence, Jane turned her steady gaze upon the Judge: young, petite and innocent, as all well knew, she looked him full in the face, and it was a look the Judge could never forget.

Slowly the party were led back through the London streets. This time the axe-man turned the blade of his fearsome axe towards his prisoners, symbolically declaring that the sentence of death had been passed on them. When Jane was back in the Tower her attendants burst into uncontrolled weeping, as they learnt that the girl they loved was under sentence of death. 'Remember,' said Jane bravely, 'I am innocent, and did not deserve this sentence. But I should not have accepted the crown.' Six months later Judge Morgan himself was dying; but one thing from which he could not escape, even to his last moments, was that fixed look which Jane had given him as he pronounced sentence. He was haunted by it: 'Take the Lady Jane from me!' he cried out in despair! 'Take away the Lady Jane!' Remorse for passing a sentence of guilt on an innocent girl drove him mad before he died.

To add to Jane's distress at this time she heard a rumour that her father, a weak and changeable character, had expressed the wish to return to the Catholic faith. As a 'reward' for his apostasy, the Queen had issued a general pardon for his part in acquiring the crown for his daughter, and countermanded the fine of £20,000 that he had been ordered to pay. His two other daughters, Katherine, a beautiful if empty-headed girl, and humpbacked Mary Grey, were given positions of honour in Mary's household and Frances too, having successfully distanced herself from Jane's plight, continued to enjoy a privileged status at court. We may have little difficulty in guessing what Jane would think if it were indeed true that her own father had bought his pardon by a renunciation of his faith.

Although sentence of death had been passed on Jane and Guilford, no one seemed quite sure when they would die. In fact, rumour had it that despite the sentence, it was still thought that Jane might eventually be pardoned. Simon Renard wrote ruefully to Charles V, 'As for Jane, I am told that her life is safe, though several people are trying to encompass her death.'

Tossed by alternating hopes and fears, Lady Jane turned yet more to the only true source of consolation to be found in Christ. A prayer recorded in Foxe's *Book of Martyrs* expresses her state of mind as she longed for freedom yet struggled with anxieties and temptations over the increasing uncertainties that perplexed her. And always before her loomed the terrifying spectre of a violent death. She feared her circumstances might prove more than her young spirit could sustain:

> 'O Lord, thou God and Father of my life, hear me, poor and desolate woman, which flieth unto thee only in all troubles and miseries. Thou, O Lord, art the only defender and deliverer of those who put their trust in thee: therefore, I being defiled with sin, encumbered with affliction, unquieted with troubles, wrapped in cares, overwhelmed with miseries, vexed with temptations, and grievously tormented with the long imprisonment ... of my sinful body do come unto thee, O merciful Saviour, craving thy mercy and help, without the which so little help of deliverance is left, that I may utterly despair of any liberty.'[2]

CHAPTER FIFTEEN

A FATAL REBELLION

Once Mary Tudor had determined on a course of action, no persuasion or advice could deter her from it. She did not trust her Privy Council even though she had picked staunch Catholic adherents to join its numbers; so took little heed of any cautions it might suggest. Narrow-minded and superstitious, Mary significantly failed to understand the people who had so enthusiastically and sincerely welcomed her to the throne. She regarded her Spanish forebears with a pitiable loyalty, even though her own people resented and suspected the connection. To make Simon Renard, the Spanish ambassador, her chief confidant irritated her councillors, but when they complained about the situation, Mary merely arranged for Renard to enter her royal apartments in disguise by some back way.

Despite Mary's distorted approach to political issues, she did sense that Renard's suggestion to marry her cousin Philip would not be popular with her people. Philip was the son of Charles V, King of Spain, who held the title of Holy Roman Emperor. He was also heir to his father's vast Hapsburg or German dynasties that extended to the Netherlands, Austria, Naples and Sicily. Linking England with this powerful consortium of nations by such a marriage would inevitably mean that English affairs would be relegated to a position of minimal importance in the priorities of Mary's prospective husband. It would also bring an influx of Spaniards into the country who might hold key positions. Little wonder then that so proud a nation as England was deeply resentful at such a prospect.

With the coronation over, and the country set on the path to return to the religious concepts that had pertained before the dawn of the Reformation, Mary began seriously to consider the question of her marriage. Her younger sister Elizabeth was a

Protestant and highly popular in the country; unless Mary herself could produce an heir, Elizabeth would inevitably succeed to the throne and undo all Mary's careful schemes to bring the country back to Roman Catholic ideals. Then there was Lady Jane still in the Tower – if only Mary could have a child Jane would no longer be a threat and could be set at liberty. But at thirty-nine years of age, Mary knew she would have to make a decision regarding her marriage soon. Names of various eligible English nobles had been suggested, but the Queen was not interested in them.

On 10 October 1553 Simon Renard, acting under instructions from Charles V, asked for an official interview with Mary. In his capacity as Spanish ambassador he now advanced the proposal that Mary should marry Philip of Spain. Torn by conflicting emotions, Mary could not give him an answer. The disparity in their ages troubled her, as did the fact that Philip was an entire stranger to her. She begged that the young man in question should pay her a visit before she made a decision, but in the royal etiquette of the times that was not an option. A powerful ruler like Charles V could not risk a rebuff from a smaller state like England. So Renard concluded the interview with a series of fulsome remarks on the character and graces of his illustrious prince, and then withdrew.

Rumours about the proposed Spanish marriage were rife throughout the court and further afield, and few could be found who approved of the suggestion. Three weeks later Renard broached the subject once again, but this time he had brought with him a formal written proposal of marriage from Charles V on behalf of his son. In the meantime Mary had come to a decision. Kneeling before the sacrament on an altar in the corner of the room, and in the presence of Renard and one other, she wept and made her response: 'My mind is made up and I can never change it. I will love his Highness perfectly and never give him any cause to feel jealous.' And for all her faults that is exactly what Mary did. She fell pathetically in love with a concept rather than a person.

News of the engagement spread rapidly through city and country alike, but was greeted with universal dismay. Her Parliament was strongly opposed to it, and even the Catholic Bishop of Winchester, Stephen Gardiner, lost his prestige with the Queen by advising her against it. Her Privy Councillors were torn between wishing to retain her favour and objecting to her plans; according to Henry VIII's will, none of his heirs could marry without the consent of the Privy Council. But when Mary's councillors tried to dissuade her from so disastrous a course of action, as it seemed from the English perspective, she threatened to take ill and die if they tried to prevent the marriage going ahead. Reluctantly they capitulated. In terms of the contract itself, Philip would rule as King of England, and Mary, as his wife, would defer to his decisions, but still retain her position as sovereign. Any children they might have would be joint heirs to the thrones of England, Burgundy and the Netherlands; if there were no child, Philip would relinquish any further claim to the English throne. No Spaniards would be able to hold positions of authority in England.

Such proposals might have seemed reasonable enough, but the mood in the country had changed rapidly from one of euphoria at Mary's accession to one charged with foreboding and anger. Fear of a Spanish takeover, together with exaggerated tales of the horrors of the Spanish Inquisition, whipped the people into a maelstrom of panic and nationalistic fury. Merchants feared that the close tie with the Hapsburg dynasty would undermine their own developing trade opportunities. Many declared themselves ready to die rather than to see their Queen married to a Spanish prince.

Lady Jane, hoping and waiting for her release, knew little of this changing situation. Security was tightened around her and her walks in the gardens of the Tower were brought to an abrupt end. Neither of her parents visited their daughter and, not surprisingly, Jane became depressed and then physically ill. As many prisoners before her had done, Jane expressed her thoughts in words scratched with a pin on the walls of her prison room –

The Queen's House at the Tower of London where
Lady Jane was imprisoned

words that reflect her troubled state of mind. Written in Latin couplets, the lines can be translated:

> 'To mortals' common fate thy mind resign,
> My lot today, tomorrow may be thine.
> While God assists us, envy bites in vain,
> If God forsake us, fruitless all our pain:
> I hope for light after the darkness.'

As a result of Jane's illness, Sir John Bridges was ordered to allow his prisoner to resume her walks within the Tower precincts, but not to see Guilford. It may well be that the young couple did meet from time to time, when the kindly lieutenant chose not to notice. He may also have carried letters between them during these weeks.

The gathering cloud of civil unrest was threatening to lead to an uprising. As the short January days of 1554 wore on, that threat turned to reality. A four-pronged attack on the capital had been planned, but with varying intent on the part of the rebels. For some it was merely to insist that the Queen renounce her intentions to marry Philip of Spain; but for others it was to remove her from the throne and replace her with the Lady Elizabeth, or even, some whispered, Lady Jane Dudley. Sir Thomas Wyatt, son of a distinguished poet, was to raise troops in Kent and the eastern counties, while Sir Peter Carew intended to do the same in the West. Sir James Croft would add to the momentum of the revolt by contributing troops from Wales.

Sir Thomas Wyatt also paid a visit to Jane's father, the Duke of Suffolk, at his London home in Sheen. Here he found another compliant supporter – despite the fact of Mary's pardon for his part in placing Jane on the throne. Perhaps, he thought, if the outcome of the rebellion was favourable his daughter might even be Queen once more. Henry Grey's role, with the aid of his two brothers, was to make a public proclamation of the causes for grievance in Leicester and Coventry, and then to raise up troops in the Midlands in support of the rebellion. All four forces would then converge simultaneously on London. Henry Grey also decided to enlist the services of his Midland neighbour and long-term rival, Francis, 2nd Earl of Huntingdon, but did so without stopping to consider whether the Earl's recent record of treachery in the case of Lady Jane might make him an unreliable ally.

Scarcely had the agreement with Huntingdon been settled before the Earl secretly reported Grey's part in the plot to members of the Council. Henry Grey was still donning his riding boots when there came a loud hammering at the door of his Sheen mansion, summoning him immediately to the City. 'Marry,' he said in exasperation, 'I was coming to her Grace. Ye may see me booted and spurred and ready to ride.' But while the messengers were being entertained to a drink in another room the Duke slipped out and made his way as fast as possible to Leicester, being joined by his brothers, John and Thomas, on the way.

On 26 January the rebellion had begun; but a skilfully planned counter strategy on the part of the government proved successful in reducing initial support for the advancing troops. A proclamation was issued, first in London and then further afield, stating that the rebels were intent upon 'Her Grace's destruction', and yet more significantly, that they plotted to put Lady Jane and Lord Guilford Dudley on the throne instead. This naturally renewed all the emotions that had gripped the country six months earlier, but, despite this, it only partially checked the rush of citizens prepared to fight under the banner of the rebel forces.

With cries of 'We are Englishmen,' Sir Thomas Wyatt's troops marched confidently from Maidstone towards London and as they went they attracted ever-increasing numbers of supporters. The Queen too had raised a force numbering 8,000 men; these she placed under the command of the eighty-one-year-old Duke of Norfolk, who was dispatched to meet the rebels as they marched up from Kent. Old and incompetent, the general was not in command of the situation, and his forces were quickly and alarmingly routed. As his men deserted from his ranks they flocked instead to the standard of 'this worthy captain Master Wyatt'. Troops from the West and Wales did not enjoy a similar success, however, and were rapidly dispersed as their leaders either fled or were captured.

Meanwhile the Earl of Huntingdon had begged the Queen to allow him sufficient troops to capture his old antagonist, Henry Grey, Duke of Suffolk. Setting out with 1,400 men at his back, Huntingdon sent a message to Grey purporting to assure him that he was on the way to join him with reinforcements as an ally in the common cause. He arranged to meet him at Coventry as they had previously planned, but he was, in fact, engaging in an act of deception and betrayal.

Reaching Coventry first, Huntingdon raised the city against Henry Grey, ensuring that the gates were closed when he and his men arrived. As soon as the Grey brothers discovered that they had been deceived, both Henry and Thomas fled in panic to Henry's property at Astley, five miles north of Coventry. Their troops, meanwhile, deserted and returned to their homes. At Astley a park keeper agreed to conceal the desperate men: Henry in the hollow of an old oak tree and Thomas under a bale of hay near the church. The other brother, John Grey, fled to Wales but was apprehended near the Welsh border. For two bitter January days Huntingdon roamed the Astley park mercilessly hunting for his quarry. Before long his dog sniffed out one frightened man under the bale of hay and at last the park keeper, fearful of reprisals, revealed the place where the wretched Henry Grey himself lay hidden. In a state of near collapse, Henry crawled out of his hollow tree and fell at his captor's feet. Once more he was a prisoner of the crown, and this time he could expect no mercy if Wyatt and his men were defeated.

For a few uncertain days the outcome of the rebellion hung in the balance as Thomas Wyatt and his troops advanced steadily on London. Yet more of the Queen's forces deserted to Wyatt as he neared the capital, and an early description of the situation speaks of Londoners who 'longed sore for his coming'. On 30

January Wyatt's forces camped on Blackheath Common near Greenwich, but the imminence of conflict caused panic on the streets of London. Women wept, shops were boarded up and a sense of siege pervaded the city. The Privy Council, ever ready to support the winning side, prepared to declare for Elizabeth. For some days rumours of the rebellion had been filtering through to Jane in the Tower. Any liberties she had previously enjoyed were severely curtailed as a strict watch was kept on her every movement. Her attendants, Mistress Ellen, Mrs Tylney and Mrs Jacob, were free to leave the Tower to purchase items for their imprisoned mistress, and they would doubtless have picked up gossip from the market place to bring back to Jane. She would know by now that her father was involved in the rebellion and realize that unless Wyatt and his men succeeded, such an act of folly on his part would probably cost her her life.

Just as it seemed that Wyatt might achieve his aim, the tide turned against the rebels. This has generally been attributed to a courageous speech made by Mary herself. Against the advice of her supporters, she determined to address the people in the Guildhall and in her deep male-sounding voice declared her allegiance to her country and urged her people to prayer on her behalf. Then in unequivocal tones she added her continued commitment to Philip of Spain: 'I consider myself his Highness's wife [even though she had not yet met Philip]. I will never take another husband. I would rather lose my crown and my life.'

Determined now to fight for their Queen and with fresh heart, the people prepared to resist Wyatt. When his forces arrived at Southwark and tried to cross the Thames at the old London Bridge, he found his route blocked. From the Tower, Jane would have been near enough to be able to hear the sounds of fighting, and to learn that Wyatt had received his first major setback. No alternative remained other than for him to march his men on up river and cross at Kingston, then turn east and march back again. But by now he had lost the initiative and his troops were dispirited and hungry with little heart left for a fight. A few further skirmishes broke out around St James's Park on 5 February, but Wyatt's men were soon overwhelmed by superior forces and easily routed. The following day their leader was captured and escorted to the Tower.

Each day of that short rebellion brought the spectre of a fearsome death ever nearer to the prisoner in the Tower. The curtailment of all her privileges was to her a sure sign that she might not have long to live. Now with news of Wyatt's defeat, that surmise would have turned to a certainty in Jane's mind. And she was right. Even though the Queen's sister Elizabeth had been most commonly mentioned as an alternative for the crown, the fact remained that Jane had once been proclaimed Queen, and her very existence constituted a threat to Mary's throne. Added to this the involvement of Jane's own father, the Duke of Suffolk, whose support in the rebellion was assumed to rest on a restoration of Jane's position, made it certain that in Mary's eyes it was no longer safe to allow the girl to live.

Even before Wyatt's final defeat, and as his men were advancing on Southwark, a warrant for the execution of Lady Jane and her husband Guilford had been signed. On 7 February the Privy Council met to conclude their decisions on reprisals to be taken against the rebels, and the first name on their list was that of Lady Jane. At Renard's prompting the Emperor Charles V had written to say that while Jane lived he would not allow his son to come to England, a fact that would weigh heavily with Mary, who found delays in her marriage plans an almost intolerable burden. A council member, Sir Richard Baker, commented wryly, 'The innocent lady must suffer for her father's fault,' and added, quoting a verse of Scripture, 'The fathers have eaten sour grapes and the children's teeth are set on edge.'[1] 'At last,' wrote Renard to the Emperor with a measure of sadistic satisfaction, 'Jane of Suffolk and her husband are to lose their heads.'

CHAPTER SIXTEEN

'I HAVE KEPT THE FAITH'

It was 8 February 1554. The city of London had fallen strangely quiet after the clash of arms and the shouts and cries of frightened men and women. Footsteps could be heard approaching Master Partridge's apartments at the Tower of London. Had Jane or any of her attendants looked out of the window at that moment, they would have seen the rotund figure of Dr John Feckenham, Queen Mary's personal chaplain, standing at the door in his priestly robes. Jane would have little illusion about the reason for Dr Feckenham's visit.

If the Queen could not save her young cousin's life, at least she could make some attempt to save her soul in accordance with her views, and Dr Feckenham was the only man Mary knew who might succeed in turning Jane back to the Catholic faith. Newly released from prison himself, where he had languished for six years during Edward's reign, the thirty-nine-year-old priest had already gained a widespread reputation for his abilities in argument. Soon after Mary's accession to the throne he had been chosen to defend the Catholic doctrine of the Mass in a public debate; his adroit performance on that occasion had been rewarded by an appointment to be Dean of St Paul's. A kindly man, it was he who had pleaded with Mary to preserve her own sister Elizabeth, suspected of implication in Wyatt's rebellion, from the executioner's block.

One look at Dr Feckenham's usually cheerful face told the hard message he had come to bring: Jane must prepare to die the next day. She and Guilford were both to be executed on Tower Hill on 9 February. 'Madam, I lament your heavy case,' said the priest kindly, 'yet I doubt not that you bear out this sorrow with a constant and patient mind.' Jane, a precocious young person, with a natural love of life and learning, and a buoyant spirit despite all her sufferings, had nevertheless thought often on the joy stored up for the Christian beyond this life. She did not react to such a message as many girls might have done in her circumstances, with a flood of tears, panic and evident distress. Instead she received her visitor with composure, for she had been living with the expectation of this news for some time. She had also guessed the further hidden purpose behind the priest's visit and said to him:

> 'You are welcome to me, Sir, if your coming be to give Christian exhortation.'

No doubt to Feckenham's surprise, the girl continued:

> 'As for my heavy case, I thank God I do so little lament it, the rather I account the same for a more manifest declaration of God's favour toward me, than ever he showed me at any time before. And therefore there is no reason why either you or others which bear me good will should lament or be grieved with this my case.'

Pressing the cause for which he had come, Feckenham began to discuss the matters at issue between Jane's evangelical persuasions and the Catholic faith. A number of questions were raised, but although Jane had received her visitor cordially enough, she had no desire to continue the debate. With only a few hours left to live, her first wish was to be alone to prepare herself to meet her God. With resolute tones she told Feckenham that her time was short and she wished to be left that she might spend it in private prayer. Rising to leave, Feckenham withdrew from the small group in the Tower and returned to the Queen. But far from admitting defeat, he was under the impression that Jane's reference to her time being short meant that if she had a few further days to live she might well be persuaded. He could even be on the verge of success.

Feckenham explained the situation to Mary, as he perceived it, and asked that Jane be given three more days before the execution. During that time he would hope to bring the girl back to the Catholic fold. Mary's reply must have come as a surprise even to Feckenham. If Jane would recant and embrace the old religion, then she was prepared to grant her cousin a complete reprieve. This was good news indeed, and we can easily picture the well-meaning priest hurrying back to the Tower with his face wreathed with smiles. All Jane must do to save her life was to agree to abandon her faith. Others had done it and gained freedom as a result, so surely this young attractive woman would be glad to avoid the horrors of death by this same means. But Feckenham had misjudged the character and convictions of Lady Jane. As he told her the news Jane listened to him in silence and then replied:

> 'Alas sir, it was not my desire to prolong my days. As for death, I utterly despise it, and her Majesty's pleasure being such, I willingly undergo it.'

Nonplussed at such a reaction, Feckenham listened in astonishment as Jane continued:

> 'You are much deceived if you think I have any desire of longer life; for I assure you, since the time you went from me, my life has been so tedious to me, that I long for nothing so much as death. Neither did I wish the Queen to be solicited for such a purpose.'

In the interval between the two visits, Jane had grappled with the terrors of death, and by the grace and help of God had overcome that dread so natural to the human heart. She had come to terms with that swift, searing pain that she must experience as the prelude to the crown of life promised to all those who are faithful unto death. Now any delay could only be an added burden. Jane had prayed earnestly that in the hour of her need God would be to her 'a strong tower of defence' and that she would not be tried beyond her ability to endure. 'Arm me, I beseech thee, that I may stand fast' had been her earnest cry, and her composure at this moment, the ultimate test of her resolve, was a clear indication that God had heard her cry.

As Feckenham prepared to leave once more, Jane begged him to ask the Queen to allow the execution to proceed the following day as originally planned. The strain of waiting was almost more than she could bear. Feckenham agreed, recognizing that again he had failed to break Jane's resolve; but he was still confident that as the hour of death approached he might yet undermine her determination, so adding to his reputation as one skilled in the art of persuasion. It is evident too that an element of human pity also motivated the Catholic priest. He knew, as did everyone else, that Lady Jane was a victim of the machinations of others: that in no way did she deserve to die. Slightly built and still so young, she stood there before him gazing resolutely at him. How grievous that she should throw life away! Why must she die? Surely, he thought, it was a measure of obstinacy that made her refuse such an offer of mercy.

When Mary heard of Jane's reaction to her clemency she was incensed at the girl's apparent stubbornness, perhaps forgetting the occasions when she too had displayed the same resolution of purpose, but in a cause far different. 12 February must remain the day of execution, but Mary did make one apparent concession. Instead of Jane and Guilford being executed together on Tower Hill, Jane would die on a scaffold to be erected on Tower Green – that very place below her window where Anne Boleyn had perished. Only Guilford would die open to the public gaze on Tower Hill. Clearly Mary feared the public disorder that would inevitably follow if the citizens of London were allowed to observe what could only be perceived as the needless destruction of two innocent young people who had taken no part at all in the recent insurrection. But before that, Feckenham must return and try again to convert her cousin.

Once more the sound of footsteps alerted Jane and her lady attendants to the return of the priest. His arrival only added to Jane's distress at this further disturbance of her inward preparations for her fearsome ordeal. But this time Feckenham had a different proposition. Would Jane agree to a public debate on the points of difference between them? In the conduct of such a debate he knew that he had excelled in the past and in his eyes it presented a last chance for Jane. But she was far from willing to face a public confrontation with Feckenham and other representatives of the Catholic Church. Jane replied earnestly to Feckenham's request:

'This disputation may be fit for the living, but not for the dying. The truest sign of your compassion for me, which you have strongly professed, will be to leave me undisturbed to make my peace with God.'

Still Feckenham would not admit defeat and after repeated persuasion, Jane agreed: the debate was to take place in the Tower Chapel of St Peter-ad-Vincula the following day, 10 February.

As a number of the dignitaries of the Catholic Church gathered at St Peter's, Jane heard news that must have added to her distress. That day her own father had been brought from Coventry where he had been held prisoner for some time and was now incarcerated in the Beauchamp Tower. Jane would be well aware that he too would probably face the ultimate penalty for treason. Although a weak and vacillating character, he had not dealt with her as harshly as her mother, Frances, and Jane felt a measure of genuine affection and pity as she thought of him.

Feckenham arrived in high spirits, confident of his abilities and anxious to demonstrate his prowess before his fellow churchmen. Certain that he would find a distraught young woman standing before him, he imagined he would be able to manipulate her successfully in order to save her life. In addition to the churchmen, Sir John Bridges, the Lieutenant of the Tower, was there to guard his prisoner; he had developed a sincere affection for Jane during her six-month imprisonment. Several of Jane's lady attendants were also there to support her.

A slight girlish figure, Jane stood facing this intimidating gathering – men all anxious to undermine her faith, and prove her wrong in her beliefs. A severe enough ordeal in itself, it must have been compounded by the sight of the scaffold being erected on the Green as she crossed over to the chapel. The proceedings opened with an obvious preamble from Feckenham:

> 'I am here come to you at this present time, sent from the Queen and her Council, to instruct you in the true doctrine of the right faith; although I have so great confidence in you, that I shall have, I trust, little need to travail with you much therein.'

Lady Jane's reply may well have added to the prelate's optimism:

> 'I heartily thank the Queen's Highness which is not unmindful of her humble subject; and I hope likewise that you no less will do your duty therein both truly and faithfully, according to that you were sent for.'

The substance of the debate that followed, written down both by Jane herself and probably by one present, can be found in John Foxe's *Book of Martyrs*.[1] First a number of clerics tried, but without success, to shake Jane in her profession and then after a long period of questioning, Feckenham took over. It is the report of his interrogation that has survived. Two burning issues divided the Evangelical from the Catholic: the basis on which a man or woman may be counted righteous before God, and the doctrine of transubstantiation, whereby the Catholic maintains that in the service of the Mass the bread and wine become the actual body and blood of the Lord. Both of these Feckenham probed with searching questions.

Jane then asserted the scriptural doctrine of justification by faith. In answer to this statement Feckenham asked the question:

> 'Is there nothing else to be required or looked for in a Christian but to believe on God?'

Jane replied:

> 'Yes; we must also love him with all our heart, and with all
> our soul, and with all our mind and our neighbour as
> ourselves.'

Feckenham thought he had caught her out and asked:

> 'Why then, faith *only* justifies not, or saves not.'

But the sixteen-year-old was a match for the wily priest.

> 'I deny that. I affirm that faith only saveth; but it is meet for
> a Christian to do good works, in token that he follows the
> steps of his Master, Christ ... [but] when we have done
> all, we are unprofitable servants, and faith only in Christ's
> blood saves us.'

Turning to the sacraments and their significance, Feckenham
demanded:

> 'How many sacraments are there?'

Jane replied:

> 'Two; the sacrament of baptism; and the other, the
> sacrament of the Lord's Supper.'

Feckenham contradicted:

> 'No; there are seven.'

Jane responded:

> 'By what scripture find you that?'

Unable to quote Scripture for his view, the priest brushed over
that issue, saying that they would discuss the significance of the

two sacraments she had mentioned. Coming to the vexed issue of transubstantiation, Feckenham began by quoting Christ's words, 'Take, eat, this is my body.' Could there be a clearer statement than this to prove the rightness of the Catholic doctrine? The sixteen-year-old knew full well that her life depended upon her reply, but without hesitation she answered:

'I grant you he saith so, and so he saith, "I am the vine, I am the door"; but he is never more for that a vine or a door. Does not St Paul say, "He calleth those things that are not, as though they were"? God forbid that I should say that I eat the very body and blood of Christ... If his body were broken on the cross, it was not eaten of his disciples.'

Feckenham made a few further attempts to undermine his young defendant, but each time Jane had the final word, and was able to declare with as much clarity as any theologian several times her age:

'I ground my faith upon God's word, and not upon the church; for if the church be a good church, the faith of the church must be tried by God's word, and not God's word by the church, nor yet by my faith.'

Queen Mary's chaplain was near defeat. Jane recorded:

'To this M. Feckenham gave me a long, tedious, yet eloquent reply using many strong and logical persuasions to compel me to lean to their church; but my faith had armed my resolution to withstand any assault that words could then use against me. Of many other articles of religion we reasoned, but these formerly rehearsed were the chief and most effectual.'

The effect of these things on John Feckenham was unexpected. A sympathetic man, he had genuinely tried to save Jane's life; and in doing so had found a strange affection for the girl springing up in his heart. With sudden meekness he confessed that despite all his learning, it would have been more appropriate if they had exchanged places that day, with Jane the teacher and he the disciple. A pang of remorse overcame him. Why should such an able, attractive young woman have to die? He asked Jane to give him some brief account of her faith, which he could keep that he might publish her faithful witness to the world.

Strangely Jane too found an unexpected warmth welling up within her towards the priest who had striven so hard to save her life. She had known few who had truly loved her in her short life. Sadly, a number in her circle who had made some profession of the Protestant faith had only used both it and her for their own ends: her parents, Admiral Thomas Seymour, and above all the Duke of Northumberland. That she should admire a Catholic priest must have been a shock to Jane herself, but as she stood within hours of a cruel and frightening death, she needed someone on whom to lean, someone to accompany her as she climbed that lonely scaffold. When Dr Feckenham, who knew that Jane had been refused a clergyman of her choice to be with her, offered to stand by her and help her in that dark moment, Jane gratefully accepted his kindness.

Yet even at so grievous a moment Jane did not surrender her sense of spiritual values, for when Feckenham took his leave that day, complaining of her obstinacy and saying that they must part in this world but would never meet in the next, she replied:

'True it is that we shall never meet except God turn your heart; for I am assured, unless you repent and turn to God, you are in evil case; and I pray God ... to send you his Holy Spirit, for he hath given you his great gift of utterance, if it please him also to open the eyes of your heart.'

By her steadfast stand Queen Mary's young prisoner had forfeited all hope of reprieve. Lady Jane would now find a place among that long and noble register of martyrs of the Christian Church – those who 'loved not their lives unto the death' – choosing to suffer rather than to deny Christ. Without doubt she had 'kept the faith'.

CHAPTER SEVENTEEN
A CROWN OF RIGHTEOUSNESS

Nothing now remained for Jane but to use the time still left to her to send her last messages and to compose her heart for the ordeal she must shortly face. But for Guilford Dudley the path was equally bleak. Only seventeen years of age, he did not possess Jane's strength of character or spiritual reserves. Although no attempt had been made to convert him to Catholicism, he had remained steadfast to the faith he had professed. But as the end drew closer his spirit broke and he began to cry uncontrollably. In the midst of his distress he had two simple requests to make before he died: both were refused. He asked the Queen that a Protestant clergyman might accompany him to the scaffold. Mary, whose bigotry overcame her humanity at this point, would not allow this. His second request was that he might see Jane once more so that they could say a last farewell. It would seem that all they had endured together had given Guilford a true affection for his young wife.

When Sir John Bridges informed Jane of Guilford's petition, she first asked after his welfare. Learning that he was in a state of near collapse, she felt that an emotional parting just before their deaths would not be helpful to either of them. Her message to him was sympathetic yet firm: 'The tenderness of our parting will overcome the fortitude of us both and will too much unbend our minds from that constancy which our approaching end requires of us.'[1]

If her own and Guilford's resolve were undermined in this way it would allow the opportunity to those ready to mock to say that their faith had not sustained them at the last. Jane concluded by begging Guilford to: 'Omit these moments of grief, for we shall shortly behold one another in a better place.' But she did agree to encourage him by standing at her window and watching him as he passed by on his last hard walk to Tower Hill.

As darkness closed in on that short February day, Jane's grieving attendants lit the candles in their bleak apartment for Jane had farewell letters to write. First she wanted to write to her father – so close by, yet Jane knew she would not see him again:

> 'Father, although it hath pleased God to hasten my death by you, by whom my life should rather have been lengthened, yet can I so patiently take it, as I yield God more hearty thanks for shortening my woeful days, than if all the world had been given in my possession, with life lengthened at my own will.'

Jane had well understood the lesson Jesus taught his followers, that it is of no advantage to a man if he should gain the whole world, yet lose his own soul.

She had heard that even at this late hour her father was filled with remorse for his folly and ambition which had been the direct cause of the sentence of death now to be carried out on his daughter. But Jane did not indulge in censure, instead she took a measure of the blame, acknowledging that she had been wrong to accept the crown. It had, however, been a sin of ignorance and, because her conscience was clear before God, she could still rejoice:

> 'Yet, my dear father, in this I may account myself blessed ... that my guiltless blood may cry out before the Lord, Mercy to the innocent!'

Jane concluded her letter to her father with memorable words:

> 'And thus, good father, I have opened unto you the state wherein I at present stand; whose death is at hand, although to you it may seem right woeful, to me there is nothing that can be more welcome than from this vale of misery to aspire to that heavenly throne of all joy and pleasure with Christ our Saviour.'

With a parting exhortation to her father to remain steadfast in faith to the end that they might meet again in a better world, she closed her letter with a benediction. In view of Henry Grey's offence against his daughter this is a remarkable letter by any standards.

This was not the only message Jane sent to her father. A small book of prayers and meditations was among Jane's few possessions: it may have once belonged to Protector Seymour, ousted by his fellow Councillors, and subsequently given to Jane, or even to Guilford, whose brother had married the Protector's daughter. Measuring some four inches in height and two inches thick, this book contains about thirty-five prayers, many of them quotations from the Scriptures, clearly selected to be of special comfort in a time of trouble. Both Jane and Guilford had read it and now they used its pages to send their last messages to Jane's father. A day or two earlier Guilford had written:

'Your loving and obedient son wisheth unto your Grace long life in this world, with as much joy and comfort as I ever wished to myself; and in the world to come joy ever-lasting.'

Bound in ornamented red morocco and now tattered with age, the book had been Jane's constant companion through these dark days. As we have seen, she had been reading from it as she walked to her trial a few months earlier. She also inscribed a more formal message to her father in the margins of another page:

'The Lord comfort your Grace, and that in his Word, wherein all creatures only are to be comforted. And though it hath pleased God to take away two of your children [herself and Guilford] yet think not, I most humbly beseech your Grace, that you have lost them, but trust that we, by losing this mortal life, have won an immortal life; and I, for my part, as I have honoured your Grace in this life, will pray for you in another.'

your grays humble daughter Jane Duddley

On that same day that Jane was writing such words to her father, Bishop Stephen Gardiner was preaching a sermon before the Queen. To bolster Mary's nerve in case she should weaken and grant Jane a reprieve, he was describing the girl as one of 'the rotten and hurtful members of the commonweal who should be cut off'. Those who knew Jane best would have found such a statement an outrageous travesty of truth. Even the Lieutenant of the Tower had grown to admire his young prisoner and was now anxious to have some small memento by which he could remember her. Sir John Bridges had been obliged to fulfil his orders from the Queen with regard to his treatment of Lady Jane, but he had done so with an unusual degree of restraint and compassion. What could Jane give him? She had very few personal possessions apart from her garments. Then she decided to bequeath to the Lieutenant that same poignant book of prayers in which she and Guilford had written to Henry Grey. Perhaps he would cross over to Beauchamp Tower after their executions and show her father the last messages from his daughter and his son-in-law, and then Sir John could keep the book for himself. No more space remained for further messages, so in the bottom margin underneath a prayer entitled 'The Songe of Austen & Ambrose', Jane wrote in her neat script a message to the sympathetic Sir John which ended with quotations from the Book of Ecclesiastes (3:2 &7:1).[2]

Little more remained to be done. Jane spent her last day quietening her heart before God, and seeking strength for the ordeal that lay ahead. She bequeathed her few personal items to those faithful, sorrowing women who had shared her last six months of imprisonment. She must choose which dress to wear for that final severe appointment, and decided that it should be the same black velvet dress that she had worn at her trial. She must prepare the speech expected of her as she stood on the scaffold. History draws a merciful veil over many of the details of the next few hours: the humiliating experience of an 'examination by a body of matrons' sent from the Queen to check whether or not she was pregnant; for even at this late hour such a condition would have induced Mary to reprieve her for the sake of an unborn child. But it was not so.[3] Some writers record that yet further pressure was put upon Jane by priests sent to 'convert' her, but they found her unmoveable still.

Then night fell – the last night of Jane's brief life. Perhaps her attendants had retired to their beds and the room was now lit by little more than the dying embers of a fire and the flickering light of the candles. There was one more thing Jane wanted to do: she must write to her fourteen-year-old sister Katherine. Maybe she was even now enjoying Mary's favours at court as one of the ladies-of-the-bedchamber, Jane did not know. Bright and carefree when Jane had last seen her, Katherine must be exhorted to think seriously about life. How could anyone tell in these troubled days what future lay ahead of the girl? Jane had no paper left, but in the back of her Greek New Testament, a book which she had just been reading for her own consolation, she discovered some blank pages. In the quiet of the room that had been both her prison and her home for the last six months, Jane began to write to Katherine on these sheets. Parts of this letter sound more like an essay than a letter, and yet in it Jane's concern for Katherine shines out:

> 'I have sent you, good sister Katherine, a book which, although it is not outwardly framed with gold, yet inwardly it is of more worth than precious stones. It is the book, dear sister, of the law of the Lord. It is his testament and last will which he bequeathed unto us wretches; which shall lead you into the path of eternal joys; and if you with a good mind read it, and with an earnest mind do purpose to follow it, it shall bring you to an immortal and everlasting life. It shall teach you to live and learn you to die.'

Even if Katherine should inherit all her father's wealth – an inheritance that would normally have come to Jane herself – she would find within this book 'such riches as neither the covetous shall withdraw from you, neither thief shall steal, neither yet moths corrupt'. As the moment of death drew ever closer for Jane, she was anxious that Katherine should be mindful of the brevity of life:

> 'Live still to die ... and trust not that the tenderness of your age shall lengthen your life; for as soon (if God call) goeth the young as the old: and labour always to learn to die... As touching my death, rejoice as I do, good sister, that I shall be delivered of this corruption, and put on incorruption. For I am assured that by losing a mortal life, I shall inherit an immortal life, the which I pray God grant you and send you of his grace to live in his fear and die in the true Christian faith.'

Jane concluded with a warning to her young sister, whom she knew to be giddy-headed and a little impetuous, that she should never swerve from the faith:

> '...Either for hope of life or for fear of death. Fare you well, good sister, and put your only trust in God, who only must help you.'

Such a message, touching and tender yet confident and unwavering, was the last letter sixteen-year-old Jane would write. Even at a distance of more than four hundred years it can take us back to that semi-darkened room in the Tower of London where a young Christian had willingly relinquished an earthly reprieve to gain a crown of life, and in doing so had triumphed over the fear of death.

She must still prepare the words she wished to say on the scaffold. Three sentences – one in Latin, one in Greek and the last in English – were found written in a daybook on the table, perhaps notes of what she wished to say:

'If justice destroys this body, divine mercy will have compassion on my soul. Death will give pain to my body for
its sins, but the soul will be justified before God.'

In the second sentence Jane continued:

'If my faults deserve punishment, at least my youth and
my folly are worthy excuses;'

and in the third she added the hope that at least,

'God and posterity will show me more favour'

– a hope that would be fulfilled in a way that the young Tudor
ex-queen, victim of the ambition of others and martyr of the
Lord Jesus Christ, could never have conceived.[5]

On the morning of 12 February 1554, Jane, ready dressed
in her long black gown, stationed herself at the window to see
Guilford pass. She had not long to wait before the small party
came into view on their way from the Beauchamp Tower. She
saw the tall slim figure of her fair-haired husband, still showing
signs of distress, accompanied by Sir John Bridges. Several other
noblemen, moved with pity for his plight, also escorted him. As
Guilford neared the window of Master Partridge's house, he
glanced upward and saw Jane standing there. Only a glance
passed between them, but it would have encouraged both the
young sufferers to remain steadfast. Guilford composed himself, and as he reached the outer bulwarks of the Tower was
able to shake hands with those who had supported him and
beg their prayers. As he mounted the scaffold Guilford managed to give a 'very small declaration' – he was in no state to
make speeches. When they bound his eyes he began to weep
once more, crying out 'Pray for me! Pray for me.' And then it
was over.

Jane remained at her lonely post at the window: her last
tribute to Guilford. She knew it would not be long before they
would return for her. Then she saw the axe-man approaching,

and behind him came the cart carrying Guilford's body. It rumbled past her window taking its sad burden to St Peter's. But the sight of the pathetic and mutilated form, roughly covered with a cloth, the severed head beside it, was more than she could bear. Tears streamed down her face: 'O Guilford! Guilford! ...the bitterness of death...', she was heard to murmur as she turned away in horror from the ghastly scene. Then composing herself Jane wrote some last words in the small book on the table:

> 'O Guilford! the antepast [foretaste] is not so bitter that you have tasted and that I shall soon taste as to make my flesh tremble; but that is nothing compared to the feast that you and I shall this day partake of in heaven.'

And now Sir John Gage, the Constable of the Tower, stood at the door. It was his duty to escort Jane on the short walk to the site of the scaffold near the White Tower. Far from happy with the mission that fell to him, he came up to the room where Jane and her sobbing attendants were waiting. According to some early accounts, he too asked for some memento of her – a token of her forgiveness for his unwelcome part in her death. All Jane had was the daybook in which she had just written those three sentences. This she gave him, and taking his arm walked down the stairs, emerging into the grey light of a chill February morning. Those who saw her commented on her dignity and serenity for she appeared 'nothing at all abashed neither were her eyes anything moistened by tears' – a startling contrast with Mistress Ellen, Elizabeth Tylney and Mrs Jacob, women who had loved her truly, and who were 'wonderfully weeping'.

Dr Feckenham was there awaiting her and Jane slipped her hand into his, glad for the human support at this moment of extremity. She had not far to walk, and was reading from her small book of prayers as she went. Mounting the black-draped scaffold, she turned to Sir John Bridges who was already there, and asked, 'May I speak what is on my mind?' 'Yes, Madam,' he replied respectfully. To the group of Tower officials, Councillors and others who had come to see her die, Jane spoke, her words steady and measured:

> 'Good people, I am come hither to die, and by a law I am condemned to the same, the fact against the Queen's Highness was unlawful, and the consenting thereunto by me: but touching the procurement and desire thereof by me and on my behalf it was never of my seeking, but by counsel of others who seemed to have further understanding of things than I, which little knew of the law, and much less of the titles to the crown. I do wash my hands thereof in innocency before God, and the face of you, good Christian people, this day...'

Her voice wavered. She wrung her hands together in distress. After a moment or two she regained control and went on:

> 'I pray you all, good Christian people, to bear me witness that I die a true Christian woman.'

Like so many other dying Christians both before Jane and after, at this last moment of life she knew of only one support for her soul, and so continued:

> 'I do look to be saved by no other means, but only by the mercy of God, in the blood of his only Son Jesus Christ.'

At that dark moment the remembrance of past sins flashed before her:

> 'I confess that when I did know the word of God, I neglected the same, loved myself and the world; and therefore this plague is happily and worthily happened unto me for my sins; and yet I thank God, that of his goodness he hath thus given me a time and respite to repent. And now, good people, while I am alive,[6] I pray you assist me with your prayers.'

Kneeling down on the hard wooden scaffold, Jane turned to Feckenham who stood by her. 'Shall I say this psalm?' she faltered. Overcome with emotion, the priest who had tried so hard to save Jane from this moment could scarcely reply. After a moment's pause, he simply said, 'Yea'. Jane then began to repeat Psalm 51 in English, David's great prayer of contrition. Feckenham knelt by her and followed her words in his Latin translation:

> 'Have mercy upon me, O God, according to thy loving-kindness: according unto the multitude of thy tender mercies blot out my transgressions... Against thee, thee only, have I sinned, and done this evil in thy sight... Purge me with hyssop and I shall be clean, wash me and I shall be whiter than snow... Hide thy face from my sins and blot out all mine iniquities... The sacrifices of God are a broken spirit: a broken and a contrite heart, O God, thou wilt not despise...'

Jane recited all nineteen verses 'in a most devout manner' and then both she and Feckenham rose to their feet. A deep silence rested over that sad scene, nothing could be heard except for the quiet sobbing of her lady attendants. Hardened soldiers who had witnessed brutality many times before stood without moving. Then with a sudden rush of emotion, Jane turned to the priest beside her: 'God, I beseech him, reward you for your kindness toward me,' she said with sincerity; then with almost a touch of humour even in that critical hour, she added, 'although I must needs say, it was more unwelcome to me than my instant death is terrible.' Erudite and skilled he might have been, but he had failed to save this fragile-looking girl from the cruel axe. Overcome by emotion, Feckenham could not answer. Seeing his distress Jane leant forward and kissed him, and for a few solemn seconds they stood hand in hand.

Turning to Sir John, Jane gave him her prayer book, the promised memento. Then she removed her gloves and gave them together with a small handkerchief to Mistress Ellen, a token of gratitude for all her care throughout Jane's sixteen years. As Jane began to untie the scarf around her neck, to loosen the upper part of her dress, the headsman came forward to assist her. 'Let me alone...' she said sharply; she wished no such intrusion at that moment. Mrs Tylney stepped forward to help her, for Mistress Ellen was too broken to do anything more. She handed Jane 'a fair handkercher to knit about her eyes', but even she failed to help the girl to tie it. As Jane stood, her neck exposed to the cold February air and the handkerchief in one hand, the executioner came forward again and this time on one knee asked the customary forgiveness for what he was about to do. 'Most willingly,' Jane replied, but as he moved she caught sight of the menacing block surrounded by straw, previously concealed from view behind him.

Almost mesmerized by the sight, Jane stood quite still until the headsman said, 'Stand upon the straw, Madam.' She moved a little nearer, and then, as the full horror of her situation swept over her, said in a low voice, 'I pray you, dispatch me quickly.' Although she knew she must place her head in the groove of the block, the girl stood transfixed. At last she spoke: 'Will you take it off before I lay me down?'[7] 'No, Madam,' came the terse reply.

Finally Jane knelt, and struggled to tie her own handkerchief over her eyes. Then she stretched out her arms to feel for the block. But she had misjudged her distance. She could not find it. She fumbled wildly. With a wave of panic she cried out, 'Where is it? O where is it?' Not a single person stirred to help the distressed victim. None could bear the responsibility of helping her to die.

'What shall I do?' that last haunting and pitiful cry has rung out over the centuries – the cry of an innocent girl – both a victim and a martyr. Eventually someone from the crowd below the scaffold mounted the steps and guided her hands towards the block. Bracing her body to receive the impact of the blow, Lady Jane called out in a clear voice, 'Lord, into thy hands I commend my spirit.' With a stroke, swift, sharp and terrible,

Jane's short life was ended. Like the apostle Paul, she had fought a good fight, finished the course and kept the faith. Henceforth there was laid up for her a crown of righteousness – a crown that none could take from her.[8]

The execution site with St Peter-ad-Vincula
in the background

Lady Jane's remains are under the flagstones between the
remains of two other executed queens, Anne Boleyn and
Catherine Howard.

CHAPTER EIGHTEEN

THE YEARS THAT FOLLOWED –
A BRIEF OVERVIEW

A short time later Jane's small frame was gathered up, laid in the cart – probably that very same cart that had so recently taken Guilford's body past her window – and trundled across the Green to St Peter-ad-Vincula. Here it was placed with little ceremony under the flagstones to lie between the remains of two other executed queens, Anne Boleyn and Catherine Howard. The historian Thomas Macaulay describes that scaffold on Tower Green as 'one of the saddest spots on earth' while Thomas Fuller, writing of these grievous events, adds quaintly that Jane 'most patiently, christianly and constantly yielded to God her soul; which by a bad way went to the best end'.[1]

A recent historian of the Reformation, A. G. Dickens comments: 'Overcome by Jane's fine bearing, historians have often forgotten to add that this execution was an offence against decency, fit to be placed alongside the worst of those perpetuated by Henry VIII.' He also points out that this circumstance 'added nothing to Mary's reputation'. Indeed, it did not. The extraordinary popularity that her countrymen had afforded to their Queen as she entered London had dwindled to virtually nothing following her proposed marriage to Philip of Spain. The execution of a young couple, who were seen by all to be innocent victims of ambitious plotters, damaged it yet further. This incident soured and shrivelled the Queen's spirit and could be said to have paved the way for that plethora of burnings of Christian men and women that has scarred her memory for ever.

The day of Jane and Guilford's execution was known for some time as 'Black Monday', for on that day, and during the week that followed, the mangled remains of many who had taken part in Wyatt's rebellion could be seen hanging at numerous London street corners. Thomas Wyatt himself was executed at the end of February. As he stood at the block he exonerated

Some of the 'Bradgate Oaks'

Elizabeth from having any part in his rebellion, and so saved England's future and arguably greatest monarch from a similar fate to Jane's. Tradition has perpetuated a story that the woodsmen at Bradgate Park lopped the tops off the oak trees in the Park as an expression of grief soon after Jane's execution. Whether this is true cannot now be verified, but certainly many of the oldest trees have been pollarded and a careful examination dates some to well before Lady Jane's time.

Lady Jane's own father, the Duke of Suffolk, was brought to trial on 17 February 1554. He pleaded that he was only doing his duty as a peer of the realm to save his country from being ruled by 'strangers' – a plea that was scarcely likely to win him many favours from Mary. Not unexpectedly, he too was condemned to fall under the headsman's axe. Weak and self-seeking, he had proved himself unstable in the hour of crisis. As Thomas Fuller was to remark of both Henry and Frances Grey: 'By snatching at a crown which was not theirs, they lost a coronet which was their own.'[2] Yet at Henry Grey's execution on 23 February, even though accompanied – against his wishes – by a Catholic priest to the scaffold, it would appear that he reverted to the faith that had upheld his daughter Jane to the end. Perhaps he recalled her longing 'that we might meet at last in heaven' and as he addressed the watching crowd on Tower Hill, he declared:

'I pray God that this my death may be an example to all men, beseeching you all to bear me witness that I die in the faith of Christ, trusting to be saved by his blood only (and not by any trumpery) the which died for me, and for all them that truly repent, and steadfastly trust in him'

– a statement from her own father that would have been worthy of Jane herself.

Meanwhile, Jane's mother appears to have been little concerned with these tragic events as first her oldest daughter and then her husband were executed. Possibly she was far more interested in a love affair of her own; for three weeks after Henry

Grey's execution, Frances, now aged thirty-seven, married their stable-hand, twenty-one-year-old Adrian Stokes, who had worked for the Greys for some years. A marriage of necessity, for Frances was already pregnant, it was far beneath her social status. She was generally despised both for the lack of respect she had shown to the Duke of Suffolk's memory and for the choice she had made. She largely retired from public life but only lived another five years, dying in 1559.

The beautiful Katherine, Jane's younger sister, had been a bright carefree girl when Jane had last seen her, probably at their joint wedding so hastily arranged by Northumberland. Thirteen-year-old Katherine had been married to the Earl of Pembroke's son, but felt the disgrace keenly when her marriage was publicly repudiated as Northumberland's plot began to unravel. Thomas Fuller has dramatized this scenario by saying that Katherine:

'...was seldom seen with dry eyes for some years together, sighing out her sorrowful condition, so that though the roses in her cheeks looked very wan and pale it was not for want of watering'.[3]

We may suppose that Jane's letter was one that Katherine read many times over in her distress. 'Good sister,' Jane had written, 'put your only trust in God, who only must help you.'

Queen Mary pressed on eagerly with plans for her marriage, although Philip showed himself far from enthusiastic and appeared to keep finding reasons why he was unable to sail for England. Simon Renard, ever at the Queen's side, constantly urged for Elizabeth's execution, using the same argument as he had for Jane's death: the throne would never be secure until the princess was dead. He also hoped that it might enhance Philip's chance of inheriting the throne of England. But so monstrous a crime against her own sister made Mary hesitate, and instead she confined a terrified Elizabeth to the Tower from where she feared that she might follow her own mother to the scaffold. Later Elizabeth was held under house arrest.

Following her marriage to Philip in July 1554, Mary's spirit became increasingly embittered, first by Philip's reluctance to spend any significant time in England and then by two phantom pregnancies which left her depressed and humiliated. Aided and abetted by Cardinal Reginald Pole, who returned from exile in Italy in December 1554, Mary began the infamous task of rooting out 'heretics' from the land. The list of honourable men and women martyred under Mary's cruel purges was carefully chronicled by John Foxe. He provides details of the deaths of two hundred and seventy-five out of the two hundred and eighty-two men, women and young people noted by Sir William Cecil who suffered the extreme agony of death at the stake rather than deny the faith of the Scriptures. At least fifty of these were widows leaving none to support their families. Heroic Protestant leaders such as Thomas Cranmer, John Bradford, John Rogers, Nicholas Ridley, John Hooper, Hugh Latimer and others were among that number, but the greater part was made up of ordinary citizens, little known to posterity apart from the small print in Foxe's *Book of Martyrs*. More than 800 others, mainly from the more privileged classes, escaped as refugees to some safer European country.

Mary's death, followed by the accession of Elizabeth in 1558, was greeted with relief by high and low alike. The noblemen who broke the news to Elizabeth that she was to be Queen found her sitting under an oak tree at Hatfield House reading her Greek New Testament. She was too overcome with emotion to speak for a few moments, but at last fell on her knees on the grass and repeated Psalm 118. 'This is the Lord's doing; it is marvellous in our eyes.' Queen Elizabeth I's compromise solution for the Established National Church is well known: the fearsome scourge of martyrdoms came to an end, and many evangelical men who had fled the country returned. John Feckenham, the Catholic priest who had accompanied Jane to the scaffold, refused to recognize the structures of the Elizabethan Church and spent the rest of his life in prison, dying there in 1584.

Nor were Katherine Grey's sorrows over when Elizabeth came to the throne. Now eighteen years of age, and not short of suitors for her hand, she appears to have attracted the envy of her cousin Elizabeth. Katherine was heir-presumptive to the throne and if Queen Elizabeth should die suddenly or if she failed to marry and produce heirs, Katherine and her heirs would expect to succeed. To prevent this from happening Elizabeth strongly recommended that her cousin should remain unmarried, and in any case, in line with Henry VIII's will, heirs to the throne were obliged to obtain the express permission of the reigning sovereign before marrying.

Katherine, however, had fallen in love with Edward Seymour, son of the executed Protector and the young man to whom Jane had been engaged before her forced marriage to Guilford. The two were married secretly in 1560 while the Queen was away from London. But when Katherine became pregnant, the secret could no longer be hidden. Elizabeth's fury knew no bounds, particularly when a son was born to the young couple. Edward was fined £15,000 and both were imprisoned in the Tower. Despite their imprisonment they managed to see each other from time to time, and Elizabeth was no better pleased when a second child was born. Although they were released from the Tower in 1563, close surveillance was kept on Katherine, amounting to little short of house arrest. She died a deeply unhappy woman at the age of twenty-eight, still under the Queen's displeasure.

Elizabeth refused to acknowledge the legitimacy of Katherine's marriage to Edward Seymour because it had been entered into without her approval; she therefore disinherited Katherine's two sons from the royal succession. As a result the throne passed from the Tudor line to the Stuart line on Elizabeth's death in 1603 – a change which led to a number of grievous consequences for the country. Mary Grey, Jane's youngest sister, who appears to have had few of Katherine's looks, but a faith and intellect akin to Jane's, fared little better. She too married against the Queen's will, was stripped of her possessions and imprisoned, dying in 1578 in her mid-thirties, impoverished and unwanted. The story of the Grey sisters is a frightening example of the control then exercised by English monarchs over the lives of their subordinates.

But the triumph of faith in the life and death of Lady Jane Grey remains a shining example of the grace and power of God in the life of one young person and deserves an enduring place in the long story of the Church of Jesus Christ.

John Rogers – minister and Bible translator – the first
English Protestant martyr in 1555
to die in the reign of Mary I.

John Bradford – writer and preacher.
Also martyred in 1555.

The fearless Hugh Latimer was burnt with Nicholas Ridley
in 1555. As they were led to the stake Latimer made a
remark that has lived down through the centuries: 'Be of
good comfort Master Ridley, and play the man; for we
shall this day light such a candle, by God's grace, in
England, as I trust shall never be put out.'

John Hooper – Bishop of Gloucester. He was told that if he would change his religious views he would receive a pardon from Mary I. He refused, saying, 'If you love my soul away with it.' The fire had to be rebuilt three times because of wet kindling due to the inclement weather and he was in agony for a long time. He was also martyred in 1555.

APPENDIX 1

INTERVIEW WITH JOHN FECKENHAM

Debate between Lady Jane and Dr John Feckenham – 10 February 1554

Jane: I heartily thank the queen's highness, who is not unmindful of her humble subject; and I hope likewise that you no less will do your duty therein, both truly and faithfully, according to that you were sent for.

Feckenham: What is then required of a Christian?

Jane: That he should believe in God the Father, in God the Son, and in God the Holy Ghost, three persons one God.

Feckenham: Is there nothing else to be required or looked for in a Christian but to believe in him?

Jane: Yes; we must also love him with all our heart, with all our soul. and with all our mind, and our neighbour as ourself.

Feckenham: Why, then faith only justifies not, or saves not.

Jane: Yes, verily, faith, as Paul saith, only justifieth. Why, St. Paul saith, if I have all faith, without love, it is nothing. True it is; for how can I love him whom I trust not? or how can I trust him whom I love not? Faith and love go both together, and that love is comprehended in faith.

Feckenham: How shall we love our neighbour?

Jane: To love our neighbour is to feed the hungry, to
              clothe the naked, and give drink to the thirsty,
              and to do to him as we would be done to.

Feckenham: Why, then it is necessary unto salvation to do
              good works also; it is not sufficient only to
              believe.

Jane: I deny that, and I affirm that faith only saveth;
              but it is meet for a Christian to do good works,
              in token that he follows the steps of his Master,
              Christ, yet we may not say that they profit to
              our salvation; for when we have done all, we
              are unprofitable servants, and faith only in
              Christ's blood saves us.

Feckenham: How many sacraments are there?

Jane: Two – the one, the sacrament of baptism; and
              the other, the sacrament of the Lord's Supper.

Feckenham: No; there are seven.

Jane: By what scripture find you that?

Feckenham: We will talk of that hereafter. But what is signified
              by your two sacraments?

Jane: By the sacrament of baptism, I am washed with
              water, and regenerated by the Spirit. And that
              washing is a token to me that I am a child of
              God. The sacrament of the Lord's Supper offered
              unto me, is a sure seal and testimony that I am,
              by the blood of Christ which he shed for me on
              the cross, made partaker of the everlasting
              kingdom.

Feckenham: What do you receive in that sacrament? Do you
              not receive the very body and blood of Christ?

Jane: I do not so believe. I think that at that supper I
              neither receive flesh nor blood, but only bread
              and wine, which bread when it is broken, and
              the wine, when it is drunken, puts me in mind
              how that for my sins the body of Christ was
              broken, and his blood shed on the cross; and
              with that bread and wine I receive the benefits
              that come by the breaking of his body, and
              shedding of his blood on the cross for my sins.

Feckenham: Why, does not Christ speak these words, 'Take,
              eat, this is my body'? Require you plainer words?
              does he not say it is his body?

Jane: I grant you he saith so; and so he saith, I am the
              vine, I am the door; but he is never the more for
              that a door or a vine. Does not St. Paul say, 'he
              calleth those things that are not, as though they
              were'? (Rom. 4). God forbid that I should say
              that I eat the very body and blood of Christ; for
              then either I should pluck away my redemption,
              or else there were two bodies or twelve bodies,
              when his disciples did eat his body, and it suffered
              not till the next day. So finally one body was
              tormented on the cross; and if they did eat
              another body, then had he two bodies; or, if his
              body were eaten, then it was not broken on the
              cross. Or, if it were broken upon the cross, it was
              not eaten of his disciples.

Feckenham: Why is it not as possible that Christ by his power
              could make his to be eaten and broken, as to be
              born of a virgin, as to walk upon the sea, having
              a body, and other such-like miracles as he
              wrought by his power only?

Jane: Yes, verily; if God would have done at his supper any miracle, he might have done so; but I say, that he minded to work no miracle, but only to break his body, and to shed his blood on the cross, for our sins. But I pray you answer me to this one question, Where was Christ when he said, Take, eat, this is my body? was he not at the table when he said so? He was at that time alive, and suffered not till the next day. What took he but bread? What brake he but bread? And what gave he but bread? Yea, what he took, that he brake; and look, what he brake, he gave; yea, and what he gave, he did eat: and yet all this while he himself was alive, and at supper before his disciples, or else they were deceived.

Feckenham: You ground your faith upon such authors as say and unsay, both with a breath, and not upon the church, to whom you ought to give credit.

Jane: No, I ground my faith upon God's word, and not upon the church; for if the church be a good church, the faith of the church must be tried by God's word, and not God's word by the church, nor yet by my faith. Shall I believe the church because of antiquity, or shall I give credit to the church that takes away from me the one half of the Lord's Supper, and will suffer no layman to receive it in both kinds? But surely I think if they deny it to us, then deny they to us part of our salvation. And I say, that it is an evil church, and not the spouse of Christ, but the spouse of the devil, that alters the Lord's Supper, and both takes from it, and adds to it. To that church, say I, God will add plagues, and from that church will he take their part out of the book of life. Do they learn that of St. Paul, when he ministered to the Corinthians in both kinds? Shall I believe this church? God forbid!

Feckenham: That was done for a good intent of the church, to avoid a heresy that sprung upon it.

Jane: Why, shall the church alter God's will and ordinance for good intent? How did king Saul? The Lord God forbid!

To this M. Feckenham gave me a long and tedious yet eloquent reply, using many strong and logical persuasions to compel me to lean to their church; but my faith had armed my resolution to withstand any assault that word could then use against me. Of many other articles of religion we reasoned, but these formerly rehearsed were the chief, and most effectual.

After this, Feckenham took his leave, saying that he was sorry for me, for I am sure, quoth he, that we two shall never meet.

True it is, said I, that we shall never meet except God turn your heart; for I am assured, unless you repent, and turn to God, you are in an evil case; and I pray God in the bowels of his mercy, to send you his Holy Spirit, for he hath given you his great gift of utterance if it pleased him also to open the eyes of your heart.

Jane Dudley

APPENDIX 2

LADY JANE'S LETTER TO HER SISTER AND HER RECORDED PRAYER

Jane's letter written in the back of her Greek New Testament to her sister, Katherine, the night before her execution.

'I have here sent you, good sister Katherine, a book, which, although it be not outwardly trimmed with gold, yet inwardly it is more worth than precious stones. It is the book, dear sister, of the law of the Lord. It is his testament and last will, which he bequeathed unto us wretches; which shall lead you to the path of eternal joy: and, if you with a good mind read it, and with an earnest mind do purpose to follow it, it shall bring you to an immortal and everlasting life. It shall teach you to live, and learn you to die. It shall win you more than you would have gained by the possession of your woeful father's lands. For as, if God had prospered him, you should have inherited his lands; so, if you apply diligently to this book, seeking to direct your life after it, you shall be an inheritor of such riches, as neither the covetous shall withdraw from you, neither thief shall steal, neither yet the moths corrupt.

'Desire with David, good sister, to understand the law of the Lord God. Live still to die, that you by death may purchase eternal life. And trust not that the tenderness of your age shall lengthen your life; for as soon (if God call) goeth the young as the old: and labour always to learn to die. Defy the world, deny the devil, and despise the flesh, and delight yourself only in the Lord. Be penitent for your sins, and yet despair not; be strong in faith, and yet presume not; and desire, with St. Paul, to be dissolved and to be with Christ, with whom even in death there is life.

'Be like the good servant, and even at midnight be waking, lest, when death cometh and stealeth upon you as a thief in the night, you be, with the evil servant, found sleeping; and lest, for lack of oil, you be found like the five foolish women; and like him that had not on the wedding garment; and then ye be cast out from the marriage. Rejoice in Christ, as I do. Follow the steps of your Master Christ, and take up your cross: lay your sins on his back, and always embrace him. And as touching my death, rejoice as I do, good sister, that I shall be delivered of this corruption, and put on incorruption. For I am assured, that I shall, for losing of a mortal life, win an immortal life, the which I pray God grant you, and send you of his grace to live in his fear, and to die in the true Christian faith, from the which (in God's name), I exhort you, that you never swerve, neither for hope of life, nor for fear of death. For if you will deny his truth for to lengthen your life, God will deny you, and yet shorten your days. And if you will cleave unto him, he will prolong your days, to your comfort and his glory: to the which glory God bring me now, and you hereafter, when it pleaseth him to call you. Fare you well, good sister, and put your only trust in God, who only must help you.'

A prayer offered by Lady Jane 'in the time of her trouble'.

'O Lord, thou God and Father of my life, hear me, poor and desolate woman, which flyeth unto thee only, in all troubles and miseries. Thou, O Lord, art the only defender and deliverer of those that put their trust in thee: and therefore I, being defiled with sin, encumbered with affliction, unquieted with troubles, wrapped in cares, overwhelmed with miseries, vexed with temptations, and grievously tormented with the long imprisonment of this vile mass of clay, my sinful body, do come unto thee, O merciful Saviour, craving thy mercy and help, without the which so little hope of deliverance is left, that I may utterly despair of any liberty.

'Albeit it is expedient, that, seeing our life standeth upon trying, we should be visited sometime with some adversity, whereby we might both be tried whether we be of thy flock or no, and also know thee and ourselves the better: yet thou that saidst thou wouldst not suffer us to be tempted above our power, be merciful unto me now, a miserable wretch. I beseech thee, who, with Solomon, do cry unto thee, humbly desiring thee, that I may neither be too much puffed up with prosperity, neither too much pressed down with adversity, lest I, being too full, should deny thee my God, or being too low brought, should despair, and blaspheme thee my Lord and Saviour.

'O merciful God, consider my misery, best known unto thee; and be thou now unto me a strong tower of defence, I humbly require thee. Suffer me not to be tempted above my power, but either be thou a deliverer unto me out of this great misery, or else give me grace patiently to bear thy heavy hand and sharp correction. It was thy right hand that delivered the people of Israel out of the hands of Pharaoh, which for the space of four hundred years did oppress them, and keep them in bondage. Let it therefore, likewise, seem good to thy fatherly goodness, to deliver me, sorrowful wretch (for whom thy Son Christ shed his precious blood on the cross), out of this miserable captivity and bondage, wherein I am now.

'How long wilt thou be absent? for ever? O Lord, hast thou forgotten to be gracious, and hast thou shut up thy loving-kindness in displeasure? Wilt thou be no more entreated? Is thy mercy clean gone for ever, and thy promise come utterly to an end for evermore? Why dost thou make so long tarrying? Shall I despair of thy mercy, O God? Far be that from me. I am thy workmanship, created in Christ Jesus. Give me grace, there-fore, to tarry thy leisure, and patiently to bear thy works, assuredly knowing that as thou canst, so thou wilt deliver me, when it shall please thee nothing doubting or mistrusting thy goodness toward me; for thou knowest better what is good for me than I do: therefore do with me in all things what thou wilt, and plague me what way thou wilt.

'Only, in the mean time, arm me, I beseech thee, with thy armour that I may stand fast, my loins being girded about with verity, having on the breastplate of righteousness, and shod with the shoes prepared by the gospel of peace: above all things taking to me the shield of faith, wherewith I may be able to quench all the fiery darts of the wicked; and taking the helmet of salvation, and the sword of the Spirit which is thy most holy word: praying always with all manner of prayer and supplication, that I may refer myself wholly to thy will, abiding thy pleasure and comforting myself in those troubles that it shall please thee to send me; seeing such troubles be profitable for me, and seeing I am assuredly persuaded that it cannot be but well, all that thou doest.

'Hear me, O merciful Father! for his sake, whom thou wouldest should be a sacrifice for my sins: to whom with thee and the Holy Ghost, be all honour and glory.

Amen.'

APPENDIX 3

FAMILY TREE AND CONNECTIONS

Lady Jane Grey's Family Tree

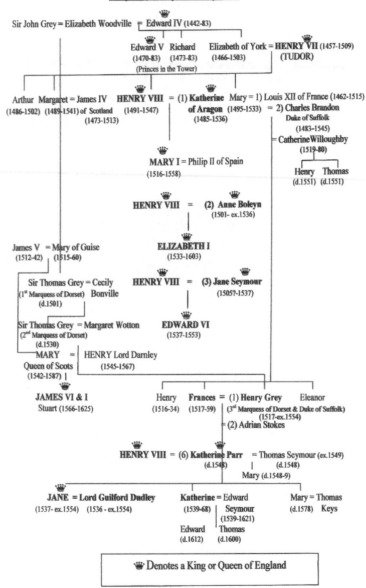

Sir John Grey = Elizabeth Woodville = Edward IV (1442-83)

Edward V (1470-83)   Richard (1473-83)   Elizabeth of York (1466-1503) = **HENRY VII** (1457-1509) (TUDOR)
(Princes in the Tower)

Arthur (1486-1502)   Margaret (1489-1541) = James IV of Scotland (1473-1513)   **HENRY VIII** (1491-1547) = (1) **Katherine of Aragon** (1485-1536)   Mary (1495-1533) = 1) Louis XII of France (1462-1515)   = 2) Charles Brandon Duke of Suffolk (1483-1545)
= Catherine Willoughby (1519-80)

Henry (d.1551)   Thomas (d.1551)

MARY I (1516-1558) = Philip II of Spain

HENRY VIII = (2) **Anne Boleyn** (1501- ex.1536)

James V (1512-42) = Mary of Guise (1515-60)   **ELIZABETH I** (1533-1603)

Sir Thomas Grey (1st Marquess of Dorset) (d.1501) = Cecily Bonville   **HENRY VIII** = (3) **Jane Seymour** (1505?-1537)

Sir Thomas Grey (2nd Marquess of Dorset) (d.1530) = Margaret Wotton   **EDWARD VI** (1537-1553)

MARY Queen of Scots (1542-1587) = HENRY Lord Darnley (1545-1567)

JAMES VI & I Stuart (1566-1625)   Henry (1516-34)   Frances (1517-59) = (1) **Henry Grey** (3rd Marquess of Dorset & Duke of Suffolk) (1517-ex.1554)   Eleanor
= (2) Adrian Stokes

HENRY VIII = (6) **Katherine Parr** (d.1548) = Thomas Seymour (ex.1549) (d.1548)
Mary (d.1548-9)

JANE (1537- ex.1554) = Lord Guilford Dudley (1536 - ex.1554)   Katherine (1539-68) = Edward Seymour (1539-1621)   Mary (d.1578) = Thomas Keys

Edward (d.1612)   Thomas (d.1600)

♛ Denotes a King or Queen of England

CONNECTIONS

Lady Jane Grey	Eldest daughter of Henry and Frances Grey
Lady Katherine Grey	Second daughter of Henry and Frances Grey
Lady Mary Grey	Youngest daughter of Henry and Frances Grey
Henry Grey	Father of Lady Jane; 3rd Marquess of Dorset and later Duke of Suffolk
Frances Grey	Mother of Lady Jane, niece of Henry VIII, and later Duchess of Suffolk
Charles Brandon	Duke of Suffolk; father of Lady Frances Grey and grandfather of Lady Jane; brother-in-law of Henry VIII and husband of Mary Tudor, Henry's sister
Mary Brandon	Younger sister of Henry VIII, wife of Charles Brandon and mother of Frances Grey
Catherine Brandon	As Catherine Willoughby married Charles Brandon, after the death of Mary. Queen Katherine Parr's lady-in-waiting, and mother of Henry and Thomas Brandon

Edward VI	Son of Henry VIII by Jane Seymour
Edward Seymour	Duke of Somerset; Lord Protector; Jane Seymour's brother and older uncle of Edward VI
Thomas Seymour	Lord Admiral; married to Katherine Parr; younger brother of Jane Seymour and uncle of Edward VI
John Dudley	Earl of Warwick and later Duke of Northumberland
Guilford Dudley	Youngest son of John Dudley and husband of Lady Jane
Earl of Arundel Marquess of Winchester Earl of Huntingdon Lord Pembroke	Members of the Privy Council

NOTES

Chapter 1 — Born a Tudor

1. Desiderius Erasmus, c.1466-1536.
2. Eusebius Jerome (c.345- c.419), secretary to Pope Damasus, had first produced his Latin Vulgate translation of parts of the Scripture in the 4th century. John Wycliffe (1324-1384), the Oxford scholar, often called the 'Morning Star of the Reformation', had supervised a translation of the Bible into English which began to be circulated in the 1380s. His work was based on the Vulgate, which had itself become corrupted over the years since Jerome's death. Numerous manuscript copies of Wycliffe's Bible were burnt in the Lollard persecutions.
3. 'I believe'.
4. Elizabeth Woodville (1437-92) was first married to Sir John Grey, Henry Grey's great grandfather. After Sir John's death Elizabeth married Edward IV and became mother of the hapless 'Princes in the Tower'. These two boys were presumed to have been murdered by her brother, their uncle, who became Richard III in 1483. Later her daughter, also named Elizabeth, had married Henry VII. This made Frances Brandon and her prospective husband, Henry Grey, distant cousins.

Chapter 2 — Lady Jane's Early Years

1. Thomas Cromwell (1485-1540) was principal adviser to Henry VIII from 1532-40. Responsible in many respects for the outward and political progress of the Reformation in England after the fall of Cardinal Thomas Wolsey, he also set in motion

the Dissolution of the Monasteries after 1534, enriching the Crown with the proceeds from the sale of the land. He negotiated the terms of the Act of Supremacy that same year, making Henry Supreme Head of the Church. With remarkable political foresight Cromwell had also instituted Henry's Privy Council in 1536 – in many ways a prototype of today's Cabinet.

2. John Aylmer, 1521-1594, graduate of Queen's College, Cambridge. Fled to Continent during reign of Mary, returned when Elizabeth came to the throne and in 1573 became Bishop of London.

Chapter 3 — Introduced to Court

1. The omission of Jane's mother, Frances, from the succession is probably because it was assumed that both she and her younger sister Eleanor would have died long before Edward, Mary and Elizabeth's reigns were over.

2. The King's elder sister Margaret and her children had been omitted from the succession because of Margaret's marriage to the Scottish King James IV. Henry had no wish to see a Stuart on the throne of England.

3. Thomas Fuller, *The Church History of Britain*, 1655, cited by J. Nichols, *History and Antiquities of Leicestershire*, Vol. III, Part 3, 1805.

4. Sir John Cheke, 1514-1557. Fellow of St John's Cambridge. Knighted in 1549. Fled to Europe during Mary's reign, but was betrayed and sent back to England in 1556, where he was imprisoned in the Tower of London.

5. Edward, son of the one who would become Duke of Somerset and Lord Protector after Henry VIII's death.

Chapter 4 — The Shadow of Death

1. Cited by J.H.Merle d'Aubigné, *The Reformation in England,* Vol. 2, Banner of Truth Trust, London, 1963, p.470.

2. J.H. Merle d'Aubigné, *The Reformation in England; op.cit.* Vol. 2, p.479, makes this suggestion, but in all likelihood this

was not Lady *Jane*, but Lady *Lane*, who accompanied the Queen at this time.

Chapter 5 — Up For Sale

1. Cited by A. Weir, *Children of England*, Pimlico, 1997, p.31, from Sir John Hayward, *The Life and Reign of King Edward VI*, 1636.
2. Published after Katherine's death by her brother, William Parr, Marquess of Northampton, it contained a foreword by William Cecil, later to become [the renowned] Lord Burleigh. The full title was *The Lamentation or Complaint of a Sinner Made by the Most Virtuous Right Gracious Lady Queen Katherine, Bewailing the Ignorance of her Blind Life, Led by Superstitions.*
3. Cited by Paul F.M.Zahl, *Five Women of the English Reformation*, Grand Rapids: Eerdmans, 2001, pp.45-52.

Chapter 6 — Plots... Plots... Plots

1. *Lady Jane Grey and her Times*, George Howard, 1822, p.157.

Chapter 7 — Political and Religious Upheaval: 1549-1552

1. Edward VI's *Treatise Against the Primacy of the Pope* can be seen in the British Library. It has recently been reprinted in *The British Josiah*, N.A.Woychuk, SFM Press, 2001, p.142ff.
2. As with 'Methodists' the name 'Lollard' was originally given in derision. Derived from the Dutch, it meant 'mumbler' or 'mutterer' of prayers; perhaps a reference to their prayerfulness.
3. Such attitudes are graphically portrayed in Eamon Duffy's recent book, *The Voices of Morebath, Reformation and Rebellion in an English Village*, London: Yale University Press, 2001.
4. Alison Weir, *Children of England*, Pimlico, 1997, p.92.
5. G. M.Trevelyan, *Illustrated History of England*, London: Longmans, 1956, p.312.

Chapter 8 — 'That Noble and Worthy Lady'

1. John Foxe, *Book of Martyrs*, Vol. II, 1875, p.1008.

2. Thomas Fuller, *Holy and Profane State*, 1652, p.294; cited in *History and Antiquities of Leicestershire*, 1805.

3. 1515-1568. St John's College, Cambridge, eventually to become Prebendary of York in 1559.

4. Giovanni Boccaccio, an Italian poet and writer (1313-1375), was famous for the introduction of the short story, particularly in his best-known work, *The Decameron*.

5. *The Scholemaster, or a plain and perfect way of teaching children to understand, write and speak the Latin tongue,* 1570, p.35.

6. *The Scholemaster*, 1711 edition, p.35.

7. James Haddon, Fellow of Trinity College, Cambridge. Refugee to Strasbourg during reign of Queen Mary.

8. *Ibid.*

9. Luther had died in 1546, four years before this correspondence took place.

10. Martin Bucer, 1491-1551.

11. *Literary Remains of Lady Jane Grey,* ed. N.H. Nicolas, 1825, p.7.

12. Heinrich Bullinger, 1504-1575. He welcomed exiles from England to Zurich in Mary's reign. He dedicated portions of his work on Christian doctrine, entitled *The Decades* to Lady Jane.

13. The above quotations from the correspondence with Bullinger to be found in *The Literary Remains of Lady Jane Grey,* N.H. Nicolas, London: 1825, p.6f.

14. Cited by John Foxe, *Book of Martyrs,* 1875, Vol. III, p.1142.

Chapter 9 — Edward and Jane – in Strength and Weakness

1. Thomas Fuller, *The Worthies of England,* ed. J. Freeman, Leicestershire, 1952, p.317.

Chapter 10 — Edward's 'Devise'

1. Sir Henry Sidney, 1529-1586. Eight years older than Edward, he was nevertheless a close personal friend. Under Elizabeth he would become Lord Deputy of Ireland and President of Wales.
2. Cited by Alison Weir, *Children of England*, Pimlico, 1996, pp.139-40.
3. Kept in the archives of the Inner Temple, London.
4. These consisted of forty-two Articles, and received Royal Assent on 12 June 1553, but were not finalized, with some revision, as the Thirty-nine Articles until Elizabeth's reign.
5. Dairmaid MacCulloch, *Thomas Cranmer*, New Haven & London: Yale University Press, 1996, p.541.
6. The fact that this prayer is recorded suggests that they, or some others, heard the words more clearly than they admitted.

Chapter 11 — Reluctant Queen

1. One account of these events suggests that Jane had been warned of the impending situation by her mother-in-law, but had not been able to comprehend it. However, Jane's own later account suggests she was entirely ignorant of the scheme that was afoot.
2. Much of the material in these final chapters has been incorporated into earlier accounts of Lady Jane Grey's life based on translations of contemporary records by several Italian writers: Michelangelo Florio, a London-born Italian, who entitled his account *Historia della Vita...del illustrissima Seig. Giovanna Graia*, 1555; Girolama Pollini's *Istoria dell' Ecclesiastica della Revoluzion de Inghilterra*, Rome, 1594; and an account by a Frenchman named René Aubert de Vertot.

Chapter 13 — Defenceless and Alone

1. This may still be seen in the British Museum.
2. She would later be granted an allowance that adequately covered her expenses.

3. Presumably Jane thought she had been poisoned at some point during her nine days as Queen.

Chapter 14 — A Prisoner of the Crown

1. Ed. J.G. Nicholls, *Camden Misellany,* Camden Society, 1850.
2. John Foxe, *Book of Martyrs,* Vol. 2, 1875, p.1008.

Chapter 15 — A Fatal Rebellion

1. Ezekiel 18:2.

Chapter 16 — 'I Have Kept the Faith'

1. See appendix for full version. The light in which different writers have depicted this scene varies according to the religious stance of the narrator. We have chosen to take a consensus of facts but follow the sequence of events described in an early biography of Lady Jane published in 1822 by George Howard, who asserts that his narrative is based on an anonymous sixteenth-century writer. The times were dangerous for Protestants, which explains why a writer remained anonymous. Account cited by Howard from the *Phœnix,* vol. 2.

Chapter 17 — A Crown of Righteousness

1. From a rare contemporary pamphlet entitled *The ende of the Lady Jane Duddeley, daughter of the Duke of Suffolk upon the scaffold at the Houre of her Death,* quoted by J.G. Nichols, *The History and Antiquities of Leicestershire,* 1804, Vol. III, Part III, p.672.
2. Forasmuch as you have desired so simple a woman to write in so worthy a book, good Master Lieutenant, therefore shall I as a friend desire you, and as a Christian require you, to call upon God, to incline your heart to his laws, to quicken you in his ways and not to take the word of truth utterly out of your mouth. Live still to die, that by death you may purchase eternal

life... For as the Preacher sayeth, There is a time to be born and a time to die, and the day of death is better than the day of our birth. Yours, as the Lord knoweth, as a true friend. Jane Duddeley.

3. Thomas Fuller in his *Holy and Profane State* (1652, p.294) perpetuated the idea that Jane was pregnant, but there is no historical evidence to support this.

4. Full text of this letter and Jane's recorded prayer is to be found in Appendix 2.

5. This incident is recorded by the early Italian writer, Michelangelo Florio (1555) and translated into English in a tract entitled *The Life, Character and Death of the Most Illustrious Pattern of Female Virtue, the Lady Jane Grey* (1714) and cited by N.H. Nicholas, *Literary Remains of Lady Jane Grey.*

6. Such a statement is thought to have been a repudiation, even from the scaffold, of the Catholic practice of praying for the dead.

7. Jane may have been referring to an alternative method of execution sometimes carried out.

8. Some details have been taken from a further pamphlet recording Jane's last days: *Life, Death and Actions of the most chaste, learned and religious lady, the Lady Jane Grey*, London: 1615, cited by N.H. Nicolas, *A Memoir*, 1825.

Chapter 18 — The Years That Followed – a Brief Overview

1.Thomas Fuller, *The Worthies of England*, 1662. ed. J. Freeman, Leicestershire: 1952, p.317.

2. *Ibid.*

3. *Op.cit.*, p.318.

BIBLIOGRAPHY

Primary Sources

Ascham, Roger, *The Scholemaster or a plain and perfect way of teaching children to understand, write and speak the Latin tongue,* first published 1570, facsimile copy, 1711.

Chronicles of Queen Jane and the First two Years of Queen Mary, especially of the Rebellion of Sir Thomas Wyatt, 1553-1554, being extracts from a pocket diary probably written by Rowland Lea, a resident in the Tower of London. ed. J.G. Nichols, Camden Miscellany, Camden Society, XLVIII, 1850.

Foxe, John, *Acts and Monuments of the Church* (known as *Book of Martyrs)* ed. John Cummings, London: Chatto and Windus, 1875.

Nicolas, N.H. *The Literary Remains of Lady Jane Grey,* with a memoir of her life, London: 1825.

The Letters of Lady Jane Grey, ed. Douglas Greary, nd.

Select Secondary Sources

Chapman, Hester, *Lady Jane Grey,* London: Jonathan Cape, 1962.

Chapman, Hester, *The Last Tudor King,* London: Jonathan Cape, 1958.

D'Aubigne, J.H. Merle, *The Reformation in England,* Vols.1 & 2, London: Banner of Truth Trust, 1962 &3.

Davey, Richard P.B., *The Nine Days Queen, Lady Jane Grey and her Times,* London: Methuen & Co. 1909.

Dickens, A.G., *The English Reformation*, London: Batsford, 1964.

Forsyth, Marie, *The History of Bradgate,* The Bradgate Park Trust: 1974.

Fuller, Thomas, *The Worthies of England*, 1662. ed. J. Freeman, Leicestershire: 1952.

Fuller, Thomas, *The Holy and Profane State*, 1652, cited in *History and Antiquities of Leicestershire,* 1805.

Howard, George, *Lady Jane Grey and her Times,* 1822.

Loane, Marcus, *Pioneers of the Reformation in England*, London: Church Book Room Press, 1964.

Lindsey, John, *The Tudor Pawn, The Life of Lady Jane Grey,* London: Jarrolds, 1952.

Martin, R.A. St.G., *The Greys of Bradgate ,* Bradgate Park Trust: 1974.

Matthew, David, *Lady Jane Grey, and the Setting of the Reign,* Eyre Methuen, 1972.

MacCulloch, Dairmaid, *Thomas Cranmer,* New Haven & London: Yale University Press, 1996.

MacCulloch, Dairmaid, *Tudor Church Militant, Edward VI and the Protestant Reformation,* London: Penguin Press, 1999.

Meroff, Deborah, *Coronation of Glory, The Story of Lady Jane Grey,* * The Zondervan Corporation, 1979.

Nichols, J., *History and Antiquities of Leicestershire,* Vol.III, Part 3, 1805.

Plowden, Alison, *Lady Jane Grey and the House of Suffolk,* London: Sidwick and Jackson, 1985.

Squires, Anthony, *The Greys: a long and noble line,* Cheshire: The Silk Press, 2002.

Squires, Anthony, and Stevenson, Joan, *Bradgate Park, Childhood Home of Lady Jane Grey,* Leicestershire: Kairos Press, 1999.

Trevellyan, G. M., *Illustrated History of England,* London: Longmans, Green & Co.,1956.

Weir, Alison, *Children of England, The Heirs of Henry VIII,* London: Pimlico, 1997.

Weir, Alison, *Henry VIII, King and Court,* London: Pimlico, 2002.

Weir, Alison, *Elizabeth the Queen,* Pimlico, London: 1999.

Woychuk, N.A., *The British Josiah, 'Edward VI, the most godly king of England',* St Louis: S.M.F. Press, 2001.

Zahl, Paul F.M., *Five Women of the English Reformation,* Grand Rapids, Michigan: Eerdmans, 2001.

---

* This is a well-written and plausible novel; a number of other novels have also been woven around the facts of Lady Jane's life, but all contain much of a fictional nature.

INDEX

OTHER TITLES BY THE SAME AUTHOR

Seeing the Invisible
'Champions of the Faith' series.
Ordinary people of extraordinary faith
ISBN 0 - 85234 407 4

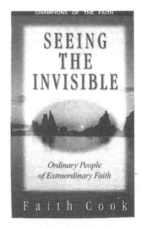

When John Bunyan asked Elizabeth to marry him he was inviting her to share not only his life but also his suffering. A heavy burden would rest upon Elizabeth's young shoulders. First there was the care of John's four motherless children. Mary Bunyan had died the previous year leaving behind four young children of whom the eldest was blind. But a yet darker shadow hung over John Bunyan. The death of Cromwell in 1658 spelt an end to the period of toleration enjoyed by those men and women who felt unable to conform to the strictures imposed on their worship by a Church of England. The threat of persecution was real. Already the small group of believers had been turned out of its place of worship; some members had faced crippling fines and all John's activities were carefully scrutinized. Elizabeth's acceptance of John Bunyan's proposal speaks highly of the charter and faith of this young woman.

Seeing the Invisible tells the story of Elizabeth Bunyan and nine other ordinary Christians who exercised extraordinary faith in their God. None of these individuals is a famous name in Christian history, but their faith in Christ and devotion to his church encourage and inspire all of us to exercise faith in the same glorious and powerful God who enabled them to 'endure as seeing him who is invisible'.

'My hope and prayer are that God may graciously use the inspiration of these ten lives... as we take a good look at the example of godly men and women, may their faithfulness instruct and inspire us.'

Derek Prime

Lives Turned Upside Down
'Champions of the Faith' series.
Ordinary people of extraordinary faith
ISBN 0 - 85234 521 - 6

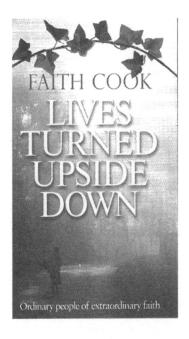

Following on from the success of her best-seller *Seeing the Invisible,* Faith Cook has again discovered fascinating and helpful stories of the lives of individuals who have been touched by the power of the gospel. This is inspirational reading for people of all ages.

'Christ's gospel does turn the world upside down. It was the wrong way upwards before, but when the gospel shall prevail, it will set the world right by turning it upside down. I put the question to you: Have you been turned upside down?'

C. H. Spurgeon

A wide range of excellent books on spiritual subjects is available from Evangelical Press. Please write to us for your free catalogue or contact us by e-mail.

Evangelical Press
Faverdale North, Darlington, DL3 OPH, England

e-mail sales: sales@evangelicalpress.org

Evangelical Press USA
PO Box 825, Webster, New York 14580, USA

e-mail sales: usa.sales@evangelicalpress.org

web: http://www.evangelicalpress.org